Alistair Shipsey

THE
MILAT LETTERS

AUSTIN MACAULEY
PUBLISHERS LTD.

ISBN 9781785547843 (Paperback)
ISBN 9781785547850 (Hardback)
ISBN 9781785547867 (E-Book)

www.austinmacauley.com

First Published (2016)
Austin Macauley Publishers Ltd.
25 Canada Square
Canary Wharf
London
E14 5LQ

Introduction

My name is Alistair Shipsey.

I am the oldest nephew (out of a family of fourteen) of Ivan Milat, the man accused of and incarcerated for the backpacker murders which took place in New South Wales during the 1990s; my mother is Ivan's eldest sister (Olga Milat). I work at a motorcycle shop in Sydney as a sales manager. We deal in Harley-Davidsons, buying, selling and repairing them.

I remember as a boy that Ivan was always someone I looked up to. He was a big, strong, fit person who always greeted you with a smile, putting out his hand for you to shake it.

He was a man of honour and had a big heart, always ready to help everybody. He was the first to help with anything. He liked his cars and always kept them immaculately clean. I even saw him with a toothbrush once, cleaning all the tight gaps in the car. He was very meticulous about things being clean and in their place.

Ivan was a very quiet sort of guy who kept to himself. He was always happy, always joked and smiled, and loved to sit down for a cup of tea. It had to be in a white cup, as he said it tasted better.

We used to have big family gatherings down at the national park on the weekends, where the whole family would gather for a barbecue and go rowing down the river together. He was a real family man; he loved his family.

We used to go bike riding together and go out to his property to shoot targets, have barbecues and camp on the land for a few days. I remember when we were sighting the guns one day, and when he let off his new rifle, it nearly deafened me.

He had quite a collection of guns: .22 calibre rifles, .44 calibre pistols, a .38 revolver, a Ruger .22, a sawn-off shotgun, a .257, an old .303 army rifle, and an AK-47. He was fanatical about his guns, and he would sit there for hours cleaning them. He used to like the black power rifles, too. I went to the Horsley Park Gun Shop with him a few times, and he would buy cartons of bullets and use the trolley to bring them out to his car.

When he was young he would take me for a run in his Ford HO, Phase Two. He would gun it up the street, smoking the tyres with the car fishtailing up the street. As a kid I was so impressed. He used to train and keep fit—he was a tower of strength. When I was growing up, I bought myself fast V8 Fords and trained hard, as I looked up to him.

He was the first to help my mother when my father died. He paid for the funeral and never wanted anything back from Mum. He was someone everybody respected and loved. He used to help everyone with his or her cars and was always good to the kids. He would always give us pocket money when we saw him, and buy us drinks and chips.

2

He was very generous and caring. He was always good to his mother (my grandmother), giving her money to pay the bills when my grandfather died. He looked after the family. If there were a problem, he would fix it. He even went down to the pub one day when three men bashed his brother, George, and battered all three of them into the ground. He left all three in a pool of blood—he's very protective of his family.

I remember my mother ringing me up in the early hours of the morning and telling me that Ivan had just been arrested for the Belanglo murders. I was shocked, as I have always known Ivan to be good to everybody. I couldn't believe it. Still to this day, I find it hard to believe he is guilty. I feel he has not been given a fair go with all the media lies and hype. But if he did do it, well, he's where he belongs; anybody who would have such a mind to do what was done in that forest should suffer the worst fate.

The backpackers were innocent people on a holiday in our beautiful country, Australia. To suffer and die in such a horrific way is so disturbing. I would hate that to happen to my kids.

I'm writing this book of letters as a matter of interest for anyone who wants to read it.

It tells you a story of his suffering and the things he has been made to do to get people to listen to him, like cutting off his finger, wrapping it up in paper and posting it to the judge who keeps knocking back his appeals. For doing it, he was locked in a little cement tomb called the safe cell for a week, with the lights on twenty hours a day.

He's been in there for twenty years now. The Geneva Convention says ten years is the maximum to put anybody in solitary confinement. He's been in there for fourteen years now. If he didn't do it, he's paying a heavy price for a

3

judicial mistake. This is why he does what he does to protest his innocence.

After reading this, I'm sure if you think he did it, then you will be happy to see he's getting what he deserves: a hard time, stuck in that cement cave to live out the rest of his life, with no life. I feel that anybody who takes another person's life should be punished to the fullest extent of the law.

LETTER NUMBER 1

From Ivan's Cell in Goulburn Gaol 1st March 2003

G'day Al,

Glad to hear from you and hope all is still fine with you and your family. Not a bad photo of your young bloke Jesse; in your office looks quite a cool lad, no doubt he impressed with your office.

That's a real beaut one of you and Alex (the president of rebels—looks like a real cool Columbian drug baron!). You all look like you're happy and enjoying the moment. I read you're happy at work, good clients and workshop. Your bike Dyno tuned and gained more grunt, which always is handy.

I note your views on women; perhaps you may have to find a deaf or blind one, as you say there are some weird ones about. I often get them writing to me, the fucken frightening things they say.

I still hear from that Margaret writing to me, though I think someone presses her start-up button to see what I say

(Margaret Patterson—I was charged with rape in 1970). It was only in the trial she revealed she never did and it was her lesbian mate (Greta). Greta hated me for fucking Margaret and talked her into sic'ing the cops onto me. This crazy sheila (in her 50s now) ever since my arrest has been writing to me, sends me weird photos. She is unbelievable.

This is why I thought if you can understand them, your book, *What Makes a Woman Tick*, would be a best seller.

Things are pretty ordinary here. The tinnitus—my hearing defect—is really getting to me at times, severe noise sending me crazy at times, makes me think of weird things.

I'll wait till Bill and co come in. I will hand him my latest appeal document to them. They will file them with the court. Of course the government will reject what I say, but I keep on about it.

Anyway, Al, thanks again. You take it easy—let it come to you. Best regards, Ivan. Hope your mum is okay.

LETTER NUMBER 2

Hello Al,

Good to hear all is well with you. Thank you for the letter received 3 Feb.

Good to know all is in control, goods in custody (money). I have read a few high court reports on that matter—depends a lot on judges' directions, can get a bit complex but you're confident so you got matters under control.

To keep occupied is the best way. You seem to have a good job, and that takes care of the day. A few good books take care of the rest, though mindful of what you say about goods in custody. It pays to recheck and figure out possible mishaps that may occur, particularly if you rely a lot on a certain thing.

I like your analysis of life as the decades went by in most cases (in the seventies, building powered, in the eighties, small business went well, and in the nineties big business grew, and in the year two thousand it all went bad—GST didn't help). The moneymaking days for small business were over, and now it's like we're in the age of extortion where because they know we need it, they charge us more. There are no friends where money is concerned.

For sure jail is okay for some, providing they are willing to learn from it. Young Kane, as you know, is on his third time around and faces a stint in Queensland when he finishes his NSW.

I used to tell him, "If you want to change your occupation and continue as you do, learn from your time." Hopefully he will now he's done this.

I've been fairly busy the last few weeks writing letters to arseholes like police minister and others regarding the police releasing information that I'm responsible for some old 1980 disappearance and letting the media convince the public that it was me.

The police often do this to me, but the last one was intense and told more lies than usual. I think it was to put a bit of shit on me as my appeal process is starting to come to the hearing dates.

Perhaps you may have noticed this time they show two photographs: the Identi-Kit one, made up from observations of witnesses who saw the man wearing a hat in dirty work clothes with the nurses that was in 1980. That photo later published in 1980 is an attempt to find me.

The other photo is of me wearing an RTA hat. I noted that the media says there was some resemblance to the Identi-Kit one.

I mainly notice both had hats on, but what was not told is my photo taken in early 1994. (I was 50 years old in 1994.) In 1980 I was 36 years old. But the idea was to frame me in the minds of the public, not to take me to court.

8

Anyway, I wrote to a few government cunts about it. I wrote a letter to one of the reporters—his article was on 25 January 2004. *The Sun-Herald*—Alex Mitchell.

The prison said no letter will be sent. I was astounded over that as to why—all I was doing is putting my side of the story forward. The fucking police don't come in to ask me a question. I couldn't get over the attitude of prison management here. Saying I cannot write to reporters—what do they think I'm going to say?

Anyway, I decided I wasn't going to argue over it. I don't give a fuck really but as long as I try. So I don't know if the letter went or not. Don't really care, as I'm doubtful they would print it.

I mainly pointed out the 14-year difference between the two photographs and asked the reporter who were the police looking for in 1980—a fifty-year-old man or what. Surely the eyewitness would have guessed his age. Anyway, I do what I can about the matter.

I was arguing about medical treatment I get in HRMU. The ombudsman recently sent me a report, dismissing my complaint. I complained the prison guard interfered in nurse duty, stopping her from applying proper treatment to me. I had a broken hand, all fingers broken. The result of guard intervention left me with a permanent deformed hand with substantial loss of use of it.

The ombudsman report said basically "tough luck," as I should expect lower duty of medical care in HRMU. Because it is the way it is. The guards dictate the treatment we get—an appalling report I'm doing a lot of arguing over.

9

Anyway, Al, it seems you all set. I'm glad you're going okay and you know how it is with others.

I would love to get *L.T.R*, but nothing can be sent in— no books, mags. I get photos, etc., at times, but thanks for offer.

R.F.F.R —yes, now I know. So best regards, Ivan 5 Feb. 04.

I'm quite happy to write.

LETTER NUMBER 3

Hello, Al,

Greetings, glad to hear all is well. Your letter was received 10/1/2004, thank you.

Unfortunately, no access to "live to ride." Actually haven't seen an issue for quite a while—perhaps someone will send me a photocopy of that page, you and the hog.

I recall early '90s. I had a live to ride magazine and you were in it then.

I haven't seen the rebel lately.

I don't associate with him and hardly anybody else, either. He is in here for whatever, and I don't involve myself with him or anyone.

I just be polite and move on.

For sure those rides you had with the club would invoke good memories: good blokes, good bikes and rest. Nothing better looking than a few Harleys together on the road, and that sound is something else. Hopefully a lot more in your future.

I guess I need a lot of luck (or a fair go would do) in my upcoming court hearings. My high court appeal now postponed, I filed a summons to the judge in chambers to seek an order I be permitted to orally argue my points before the hearing.

The issue I rise in this summons has to be finalized before appeal hearing can be heard—as to what happens depends on my summons issue.

I am sure once this order issue is heard, my appeal will soon be back on. I am sure government similar to that shit early last December will put out more bad publicity.

Still no police see me yet. I wrote to Commissioner Moroney about his arsehole police methods. I doubt if he will reply to what I said to him.

Thanks to the thoughts you have on life and things (your two-page, typed-up submissions). Control one's own mind and things all okay. I always do that, though at the expense of my own body, but when there is no future, it's easy to do willingly.

Anyway, Al, thanks again. I'm always glad to hear from you, and you seem to be going okay. Stay cool—it's not only other prisoners who can be arseholes.

Till next one, my best regards, Ivan. 11 January 2004.

LETTER NUMBER 4

Two Pages from Ivan at "CARRS CASTLE" HRMU 9 Goulburn Prison 5th February 2004

Hello Al,

Good to know all is well with you. Thank you for the letter received 3 Feb.

Good to know all is in control. Goods are in custody. I have read a few high court reports on that matter—depends a lot on judges' directions, can get a bit complex, but you confident so you got matters under control.

To keep occupied is the best way. You seem to have a good job, and that takes care of the day. A few good looks takes care of the rest, though mindful of what you say about goods-custody—it pays to recheck and figure out possible mishaps that may occur, particularly if you rely a lot on a certain thing.

I like your analysis of life as the decades went by in most cases. Yes, depends a lot on one's own style and

13

ability to recognize others. Overall, you're right—most things go down the gurgler if you rely too much on others.

For sure jail is okay for some—providing they're willing to learn from it. Young Kane is as you know on his third time around and faces a stint in Queensland when he finishes in NSW.

I used to tell him, "If you don't change your occupation and continue as you do, learn from your time." Hopefully he has done this.

I've been fairly busy the last few weeks writing letters to the arseholes like the police minister and others regarding the police releasing information that I am responsible for some old 1980 disappearance and letting the media convince the public it was me.

The police often do this to me, but last one was intense and a lot more lies than usual. I think it was to put a bit of shit on me as my appeal process is starting to come to the hearing dates.

Perhaps you may have noticed this time they show two photographs, the identikit one – made up from observations of witnesses who saw the man wearing the hat in dirty work clothes with the nurses, that was in 1980, the photo later published in 1980 is an attempt to find him.

The other photo of me wearing RTA hat, I noted media says there was no resemblance to the identi kit one.

I mainly noticed both had hats on, but what not told is my photo taken in early 1994 (I was 50 years old in 1994).

In 1980 I was 36 years old, but the idea was to frame me in the minds of the public, not to take me to court.

14

Anyway I wrote to a few government cunts about it, I wrote a letter to one of the reporters – this article on the 25 January 2004, sun herald – Alex Mitchell.

The prison said this letter won't be sent. I was astounded over that as to why—all I was doing was putting my side of the story forward. The fucking police don't come in and ask me questions. I couldn't get over prison management here saying I cannot write to reporters. What do they think I'm going to say?

Anyway, I decided I wasn't going to argue over it. I don't give a fuck really, but as long as I try, so I don't know my letter went or not, don't really care as doubtful they would print it. I mainly pointed out the 14-year difference between the two photographs and asked the reporter who the police were looking for in 1980—a fifty-year-old man or what. Surely the eyewitnesses would have guessed his age. Anyway, I do what I can about the matter.

I'm also arguing about the medical treatment I get in HRMU.

The ombudsman recently sent me a report, dismissing my complaint; I complained that prison guard interfered in nurse duty – stop her from applying proper treatment to my broken hand, all fingers broken.

The result of guard intervention left me with permanent deformed hand with substantial loss of use of it,
The ombudsman's report said, its basically bad luck, as I should expect lower duty of care in medical care in HRMU.

Because it is the way it is – the guards dictate the treatment we get – an appalling report, I'm doing a lot of arguing over it.

15

Anyway Al, it seems you're all set, I'm glad you're going OK and you know how it is with others. I would love to get LTR but nothing can be sent in, no books no mags, I get photos etc. at times, but thanks for offer. R.F.F.R. yes now I know so best regards, Ivan 5 Feb. 2004. I'm quite happy to write.

LETTER NUMBER 5

Two Pages and 2 Page Copy of Carr's Letter from Ivan at "CARRS CASTLE" HRMU 9 Goulburn Prison 1st March 2004

Al, greetings,

I'm glad to hear from you, and thank you for the mail received 28 Feb. I hope all is fine with you.

In spite of the feelings you may have regarding your recent court hearing, particularly Joe's failure, when it comes down to it, family is all you can count on—particularly your mum. They basically will die for you in the effort they put in.

I only know a little of how the business works—the court process. RE proceeds—suspected to be proceeds of crime. I believe it's a one-way street as far as they are concerned. One has to be very persuasive and have the proof to come out ahead.

17

And it never surprises me on your business enterprises. It always included you to go first class—the little I know was that I recognized you did it right and conducted yourself well. The good thing, Al, you still got the opportunity.

I know you're aware you have. Forgiveness is good, but never let them again have the chance to error. Keep that attitude—for sure you have to raise your young bloke, it's the only way to go. To explain the pros and cons of the various ways and go for the goal that puts them on top, look at all the successful family companies handed down from generation to next—their aims never alter.

At the moment I'm on a protest here. I started on 25 February a hunger strike (I'm bloody well hungry). No food eaten, only drink—water, coffee. I'm too old for this shit and my body is in poor shape—particularly as I've done it before (to get anything, this is what I have to do). This time it's only about the Carr government's continuous attacks on me simply to further discredit me (if that's possible). I'm more concerned the effort on my High Court appeal is reason I embark on this protest.

As you know, recently the court refused me permission to speak to the upcoming hearing to explain my points. Perhaps my written submissions were not persuasive enough. (I wasn't allowed to attend the hearing and had to rely on written submissions.) I'm no lawyer, not even a jailhouse one. I do my best.

Anyway, Al, no doubt you will hear more about my protest. Government authorities will rubbish the fuck out of me for it. I enclose a letter (copy) I recently sent to "Premier Carr" about my protest and why (I can type very slowly). Have a read and see what I'm about. (Letter referred to at beginning of book.)

18

So thanks again. I'm always glad to hear from you.

Best regards, Ivan. 1/3/04

LETTER NUMBER 6

Two Pages from Ivan at "CARRS CASTLE" HRMU 9 Goulburn Prison 22nd March 2004

Hello Al,

Giddy, thanks for the letter. It's good to know you going okay—head cook sounds okay.

I read your type-up page regarding what makes a woman tick. And your plans to hopefully publish such a book via the Net.

That's good. If you really have it in your mind, it could be a success—go for it. Don't let others say, "What do you know?" or "It's a waste of time, others have done it." Till you run with it, you don't know.

I see at odd times on TV someone interviews an author. Recently on *60 Minutes* (I think?), a bank robber wrote a book. He's on TV—your idea is bound to attract attention. As your subject is a complex matter, you may have discovered how they do work. Good luck.

As you know, I came off the anti-food protest (you being head cook wouldn't approve of non-eaters). Only went 18 days, but it knocked me about.

It's been a week totally I've been back on food. Still hurts me at times—body made it plain to me, I'm really fucking myself in what I do.

As you know, I just got plain sick of them having a go at me, blaming me for the murder-body-disappearance—always those government cunts doing it.

Police, MPs and anytime I complain, no one interested, so I sent a lot of letters—no reply, so for the letter to Premier Carr, I sent copies to everyone else and kept it up that the government is trying to murder me to shut me up.

Police came out on 19th day. They were very insistent my anti-food protest did not lead them to come see me; they told me this a few times.

Well I don't think so. I think seeing that was the cause of it—why I went on hunger strike on what they fail to do. They were told to come out to resolve the matter. It was getting a bit dangerous for everybody—me and the government. What if I did collapse and die, and they let it happen. I had a strong website going on the outside—Justice Action. Put one out and printed up my letters on it, why to stuff my high court up.

I raise I'm being framed for Belanglo—they don't want me to get a hearing in high court.

The police—all they ask me is where I was on 12 July 1980! That's when the two nurses were last seen. Well, I had no idea where I was. It was a Saturday evening, they said. I was probably at home with Karen and young Jess. If

21

I'm not at work, I'm with them. I knew I was in the "Tollgate Hotel drinking with two nurses."

The police did not tell me a lot but did say a prisoner seen me here in Goulburn Prison in 96-97, and he said he recognised me as the person drinking with two nurses on 12 July 1980. He did not report it till '03—this is what police said, no idea of who the prisoner is.

So police said they would put in and see what happens! I don't fucken care what they do; I'm fed up with the pricks and will see what happens—but not worry about it.

Anyway, Al, that's how it is with me. Do your own thing and look out for your young son.

Not much more is really necessary. Make yourself comfortable with what you are doing, show your young bloke the way—he can see which way, especially with a guide. So good to hear from you again.

Best regards, Ivan. 22/March/04.

LETTER NUMBER 7

Two Pages from Ivan at "CARRS CASTLE" HRMU 9 Goulburn Prison. 11th April 2004

Hello, Al,

Hope all is fine with you. Thank you for the letter and photographs given to me on 10 April.

The club looks all right (photos of it) and a fair size generally one does not see what inside—previously. I've only seen outside as media reports on a raid conducted by police

A C3 easy for you, never for me. I used to always be A2 classification—that's maximum security. But once this place opened to perpetrate the propaganda they raised, I (not told of this at time) was given an A1 rating, about as low or worse I can get.

I continuously ask why but never get an answer—no wonder I think they're a pack of areoles. I think you realise you have to go along with them, let them cure—correct—

your faults? With women? It's just as well you did not say Henry the VIII had the right idea in how to deal with women.

If your book has to go on hold to satisfy them so no rocking the boat, so it has to be. You have to recognise the priorities of the place.

I don't think any of us knew where it was—besides somewhere at Dubbo!

As you know, I have never been there. I can only guess the police were desperate to find someone to connect me to the. They police raided a few other places once it came known I had known them.

I'm pretty sure you would now have difficulties ever visiting me—in the past it was different. Anyway, I don't think I will be greatly concerned about visitors if my High Court appeal goes down the gurgler. I noticed recently that it will be heard on 30 April at Sydney.

I'm not allowed attending, and it is dependent on my documents I have put forward. Naturally I won't accept a dismissal.

I have no problems getting photographs—the odd magazine page or two (like that LTR pages). They won't give me any large quantity of pages or a book (legal documents only excluded). I found out recently when I was sent a copy of one of those books about me—it was withheld, returned to sender.

If you get your book published, I'm sure extracts will be published in papers and you will be interviewed on *Sunrise*, TV, etc., especially on the topic you raised.

24

Tell your mum not to get too excited about what others have done. It has happened and little can be done now about it (I refer to Shirley buying her Queensland unit-veronica-Paul). I don't need her worrying herself sick, getting all upset about it. I know what she's on about—but fuck them.

[Ivan's sister Shirley took Ivan's share of the house money when it was sold, instead of giving it to him for his trial, and brought a unit up Queensland and left it to her daughter when she found out she had cancer.]
Anyway, Al, great to hear you're okay. Stay cool, Ivan.

LETTER NUMBER 8

Two Pages from Ivan at "CARRS CASTLE" HRMU 9 Goulburn Prison 2nd May 2004

Giddy Al,

Good to hear from you. Your letter was received 1 May, thank you. You appear to be going okay.

I'm not sure if you were aware I was supposed to have my leave application heard last 30 April; I had psyched myself up, readied for a poor result.

I had no intention of accepting a dismissal of my appeal, but High Court registry sent a fax, received last Thursday, 29 April, informing me my appeal application was relisted for hearing on the 28th of May.

There was no details why such a change was made—I tend to think that the judges are having difficulties in getting over my arguments? (Well, they could have!) Anyway, so now I wait till 28 May.

26

I am sure Henry always had a lot of steps ahead of them, I am not aware of the documentation (regarding Henry) in the investigation of my matter. I did not see any—which does not surprise me. Why should there be? The police at that time would have travelled anywhere to get something on me. Or to implicate others as part of it.

Anyway, at least you are going okay, that's your goal, till your address returns to normal.

Though as you know, there are a lot of wackos out there as well. A lot of them write to me at times. I tell you, Al, there are some real people out and about.

In the meantime I just cruise along. I enjoy myself by replying to those arseholes who ran NSW ombudsman office—those pricks would sell their own mothers, as they are a subsidiary of Carr Services. I never expect them to address any concern I put to them.

They apply but never allow me to win, so I keep going on and on, asking them to look at it again.

So anyway, Al, you appear to be going well (be aware of trick surprises)—keep at it.

I see that Rossi (Moto GP rider) is going good as well; the only way that he will lose is if he changes to Harleys (not that HD has to race). I always watch the Moto GP.

So, Al, stay well. Thanks for writing—my regards, Ivan 2/May/04.

LETTER NUMBER 9

Two Pages from Ivan at "CARRS Castle" HRMU.9 Goulburn Prison 17th May 2004

Hello Al,

Giddy, I hope all is fine with you and family.

Thank you for the letter received the 16th.

It does appear you're going quite well on the job at Joe's and doing a fair bit of business for him.

I'm not surprised at your business sales expertise—I recall your business at Coffs, well run and in the middle of town. That was quite an achievement, I thought—a lot of people would never attempt to do something like that.

I am sure if you had the right incentive behind you, and Joe could see it—he could take a six-month cruise somewhere and leave it to you, to reorganise his business, give you the power and resources, and six-odd months later I think you would (if you had the right incentive) really put his place as one of the most best shops around.

But don't you approach him—see if he can recognize what you are capable of.

Otherwise learn a bit—think a lot and you may wish to open your own business up down the road?

I note your comments concerning my circumstances, thank you. I'm doing my best, but I'm aware the High Court can simply explain away. Who would question the wise old judges of the High Court?

I do. I wrote to the high court judge (mc Haigh j) who determined that application on 24 Feb 2004.

I asked to be able to orally argue my appeal case— McHugh J said no. He wrote up a lot of shit about my application. I pointed this out—I don't think he actually got my letter. I got a letter from the High Court telling me High Court judges don't reply to applicants, so I wrote with another six pages to them.

Now, don't go getting concerned about me. Between this place, HRMU and whatever the High Court result is, I'm about fed up and cannot see me hanging in for much longer. I've been fed up with lies they tell me for quite a while and with the mind games they play, I really don't give a fuck about much anymore.

Yes, I realize your mum's views really got her going— as I said, it does get to me as well. I rely on appeal battles to keep me in track, that good near on over, I'm ready for anything.

I'm aware of those books—to date never really seen any of them. I believe a few of us mentioned some parts of it—how it was put (usually all wrong), but I think the idea was as long as it sounds okay.

I see in the papers the new triumph bike a 2.3 litre machine—very large. $25.000, I believe the price is. It

29

looks good—photograph of it in the paper. The article mentioned Honda and Suzuki—their cruisers have bigger motors than Harley. The point they fail to realize is they tried to be like Harleys, but no one has ever succeeded, and the latest Jap stuff won't, either. But a smart-talking salesperson who knows his bikes no doubt could steer a potential Harley buyer into buying one.

They certainly look impressive. No doubt the triumph will have some mechanical defects; the Japs always seem to look ratty and cheap after the next model comes out.

Anyway, Al, I'm glad you're going okay, and it appears you on track—on top.
Keep an eye on the ball and wait for your time.

By time you get this, it will be close to the 28th of May, so it will be known then. I'm ready for it.

Thanks again. My best regards, Ivan 17/May/04.

LETTER NUMBER 10

Two Pages from Ivan at "CARRS CASTLE" HRMU 9, Goulburn Prison. 4th June 2004

Hello, Al,

Greetings, glad to hear from you. I see all appears fairly well with you, and in the circumstances that's all we can hope for.

As you know, the high court dismissed my appeal on 28 May. So far I don't know no reasons they used to overcome my case; it's plain they wasn't impressed with my arguments. I await to receive their judgement. It appears they take their time to write up this document.

Anyway, I won't be accepting this. I find it difficult to accept they could legally overcome the principles I put forward, and I believe they rely on the prestige and respectability of the high court to give weight to their decision.

I have already indicated to the relevant authorities, I will be arguing the High Court decision and have taken some steps to find out the procedure necessary.

To attempt to get a review—an inquiry into the process.

I read that bit in the paper about Richard. I wondered why it appeared and was happy enough with what (I thought) he said. I was not too surprised with my result; I realise they cannot allow me to win.

I had written before the appeal on 28 May to the High Court. One letter to the judge who said it would not be unfair if I was not present at my appeal. I told him (McHugh J) that he was wrong; he assumed a lot upon what I would do or say—his decisions are based on his opinions and views, not of legal reasoning. The judge did not reply, but I got a letter from a senior person from High Court saying the high court judge don't reply to applicants.

I sent a five-page letter to the High Court expressing concern at the procedure used by the high court. This was sent on 16 May (before the appeal on the 28th).

As you say I got rail roaded. The high Court covered up the matter. There is no one at the hearing to look after my interests; it's held behind closed doors.

They release the decision, then it takes weeks before one gets the details. The details are carefully written up; it is not like a regular court hearing—no recording of procedure as it happens. I will do my best to bring this matter to light. This case my story continues on still. I think the pricks probably thought it was the end.

I only get my information about bikes from what I read in the papers. I realise this does not really say too much; I am sure any one of them is okay. But I don't think they will outsell the Harley, or really get the attention as Harleys get.

I hope all is well with your mum; no doubt she may appear to say my lack of proper legal (funded) counsel was my problem. I don't think so—it's extremely difficult to win High Court appeals, whether with counsel or not. They plainly had no intention I would be allowed to win.

It's not unusual to get high court judgement overturned. A review depends solely on the affected party. It's difficult, particularly for me, as the government will resist my assertions strongly. I accept this.

Anyway thanks again. A pity I could not give you news that was good for me, but don't wipe me off yet. I have no intention of not fighting it.

You take care. Keep an eye out. I'll catch you again. My best regards. 4/June/04.

LETTER NUMBER 11

Two Pages from Ivan at HRMU 9 Goulburn Prison. Goulburn 2580. 18th November 2004

Hello, Al,

Glad to know all is fine. I had heard you were okay; hopefully I can acquire the mail you posted.

As you are aware, I was prohibited from receiving or sending mail to you once you gained that outside job. Some security issue.

I could have done this or that or you this or that; naturally I was totally mystified by the reasoning, but the more I protested, the more they were convinced something could occur. This was not caused solely by you or me; it appears it really only applies to this place.

I do recall quite well that accident 20 years ago! Down Bulli ways—you laid up for a while. Unfortunately now it is catching up with you. But there is some remarkable medicines about. I've got arthritis—legs as well as you say, unbearable pain—you feel if you had an axe you would cut your own leg off at times. I get a little pill a day—unreal how it does the job.

I guess you may have seen the Warthog story recently. I'm not sure when you posted your letter (I received it the 18th—thanks).

Bill and Carolynn and others done their best. Normally it would have been there story—how my arrest and conviction affected them and others. Well, all they were was reasonable things about me; for sure any copper that was available would say what one would expect. I was aware Warthog was speaking to them—ABC wrote to me for my views and mentioned they were talking to him.

I said nothing much and referred that issue to talk to Bill and co to get a proper view. I assume they paid him some cash and wrote up his story for him. I'm a bit disappointed at ending—my phone calls to Carolynn were altered, but I suppose they had to portray me like that.

Don't you ever wonder—I do—why they determined to put it in the minds of everyone I'm as guilty as hell; it appears they will never consider a review on me. I am continually writing to high court, failing to properly determine my case; of course they don't like me pushing the issue. Anyway I do my best. I always reply to those shithead politicians who write up stories in the media.

I was recently told that some ex-crim recently written a book about his story— smuggled heaps of cash out of Africa in the early '90s! I never met him—bloke named Dutton. I was told it appears he wrote a book on his adventures and the cash (couple plus millions), and there is a chapter about when he was in Long Bay Prison. The story goes he roomed with me, as he was a calming influence on

35

me. That I used to fly off the handle a lot, he used to calm me down. The story was in the Australian newspaper a little while ago!

I didn't see it but was told about it. I never met or knew this Dutton! And I am very choosy whom I roomed with then, and still am.

I supposed that arsehole Dutton fit me in his book because he knew it would create interest. Marsden did the same thing in his book, and that got him a full page in the *Herald*. No one referred to what his book was about, but they sure paid a lot of attention on what he said about me. It's like the "Warthog" people will automatically assume it's true what he says.

I'm not sure if you are aware of Warthog history, but where the name "Warthog" originated from, how the name came about, was your dad raised it in the middle '60s. He put it on "rare" Marilyn (Boris's wife). I'm not sure what did occur; it was nothing serious, but from then on we (the boys) put the name on Boris, and it's been with him ever since.

Anyway I'm not sure if you really know how the "Warthog" is, but the best thing I can tell you is never let him know what you are doing.

Anyway it appears you going okay. Glad to know you're taking care of your mum. Actually it was only a couple of days ago I received a letter from her—I sent a reply, of course.

So I'm still doing what I have to do. Probably end up in the D Ward next. Till then, I drink coffee and attempt to prove my innocence.

Regards to all, Ivan 18 November 2004.

LETTER NUMBER 12

One Page from Ivan at HRMU 8, Goulburn C.C 2850. 16th January 2005

Hello Alistair,

Hopefully you and the family are fine. I received your letter today, 16 January. I noticed the postmark on the letter says "13 December '04." For unknown reasons on occasion my mail is held up; only a few days ago a letter from Glen Dhu dated 21 November '04 was finally given to me on 14 January!

Anyway this happens. I guess by now you would be feeling a lot better regarding the repair of old injuries. Those things do catch up with you; thankfully there is some good gear about to relieve the pain. No doubt your doctor prescribes this.

(For sure the Warthog was disappointing, but that would be expected from him; it's the arsehole TV producer who set up the whole thing, ambushed Bill and Carolynn. It was supposed to be their story.

No doubt the TV mob paid the Warthog and wrote up the script. One could think why they still pursue this—to deliberately target me after all these years. Are they afraid I may convince someone it wasn't me?

Anyway the cunts will always be there, and I will always be arguing my case. I about nearly finished the review of conviction petition; of course I'm aware the government courts are not interested in what I've got to say and they use their bullshit to dismiss – ignore whatever I say. But till I die, I will never go away from what I do.

Good to know your business is going okay. I see on the news on vehicle sales in '04, 3600 Harleys (new) sold in Australia, that figure always increasing, I'm not surprised at your success on this, and no doubt others are aware of it.

I hear Dick is going okay, got a Harley as well, which puts the wind up people. I hope your mum's okay; I received her mail-card, replied via her PO address. Anyway, we still cannot receive things—books, etc. Thanks anyway.

I wish you well as always. Best regards, Ivan 16 January 2005.

HRMU 8 exactly the same as 9.

LETTER NUMBER 13

One Page from Ivan at HRMU 8 Goulburn C.C. Goulburn 285026 January 2005

Alistair,

Greetings, it is good to know you are going okay and recovering, all a bit painfully slow, unfortunately. Thanks for the letter dated 22 Jan. Surprised I received it on the 26th.

I assume you are covered by medical benefit funding? I see you doing a lot of reconstruction on yourself. A lot of people don't voluntarily do this; they wait till the body breaks down and then have a hell of a time getting repaired.

The dental work is expensive, always has been, but as you know it's quite technical and needs experts—well-trained ones—so the cost. A lot of people hate dentists—I always have. I probably need all that work on me which you are getting. That's good to get knocked out—won't feel a thing, and painkillers later on take care of what follows.

Back in the middle to early '70s, I got a bit of work done; they used a sort of laughing gas in these times—quite good, actually no pain. I mentioned this to Dick and co. They paid a visit and helped themselves to the gas; they used it for a week—works just like grass.

No doubt Warthog got paid a bucketful of cash. In some cases it's unreal what they pay; I couldn't believe what they paid (*Woman's Day* magazine) young Lysine— her story "*Ivan's My Dad*". She only found out after my arrest and rarely seen, yet they paid her a heap. I don't know what she told them—would make a reasonable story. She should be one of your subjects, or who ever read her story to see what possesses them to read that stuff. This is probably why your future book will sell, if can halfway discover their minds.

I'm extremely glad to know your mum (DI) appears to be recovering okay. At least with my being slammed up in here, there is no chance of me wearing anything out—it's probably decaying a real lot, but I hardly notice.

Anyway thanks again. Stay cool and do what you do best.

Best regards, Ivan 26 Jan 2005.

41

LETTER NUMBER 14

Two Pages from Ivan at HRMU 8 Goulburn C.C. Goulburn 2580. 21st February 2005

Hello Alistair,

G'day, good to hear from you and things are going along okay. Your letter dated 13 Feb was received the 19th, thank you. I can guess the ironwork strapped on your leg causes considerable discomfort; hopefully you can use it for your advantage—beside it being there to support you while the old bones knit up.

I imagine real keen kids would be wrapped working in a bike shop, even just for the work experience. As you know if they keen then at that age, they are generally hooked.

I remember Paul when he was about 11 to 12 years old; as soon as a bike came in the place (Campbell Hill Road), even if he was having tea, he was up and out the home— used to drive Mum crazy. That's how he learnt a bit about them. Things no different with kids these days either—

good to see you taking advantage of it; it makes your job better and does help them as well.

I see in today's paper (tele) bike sales at record highs—so is car sales as well.

Dentists always been expensive, that's why they so expensive—they do a good job with no real pain, and once you get the work done you can really feel and see the difference.

I get my share of women, writing to me—some real good-looking ones, too (if it's their photographs they're sending). For some reason they all say they around 20 to 30 years old, though their writing suggests they're much older.

I'm very careful in my replies. I'm not real keen on writing to young ones. If you get your book up, you have to devote some chapters on what and why they write to prisoners, and weirder is that sheila—I got charged for rape—in 1970. At the trial she ends up saying she never was complaining but her friend (Greta), who was a lesbian, she was the one who talked Margaret into screaming rape. I only raise this as that Margaret ever since my arrest been writing on and off to me. I hardly reply, but she keeps on coming, sent me a card only last week.

I remember after the trial in 74, I never seen her again or heard from them. When I got arrested in 1994, Margaret started the writing the first letter she sent said, Greta still hates you.

If you can work out how they think, you will be the first one. If they love you, they will let you. Of course most complain—but some think its great!

43

The lebs basically appear to run most things this days—crime-wise. A lot in the prison system and quite a few join them. I had no idea they're into bikes; I imagine it's not bikes but the distribution or whatever—the sales?

I guess you know what I mean. What I do notice, they can do okay but they're not real smart for any length of time. I don't get involved with them (or anyone in here). I do my own fucken thing and don't give a fuck what they do; I know they are as deadly as anyone else can be.

Anyway, Al, I battle on but hardly think I can cop much more of this place. More difficult to do—I've told them but as you know, they don't take no notice; I don't give a fuck either.

So thanks again and take care. Regards, Ivan 21 Feb. 05.

LETTER NUMBER 15

Two Pages from Ivan at HRMU 8 Goulburn C.C. Goulburn 2580 18th April 2005

Giddy Al,

Good to hear from you. Your letter arrived 16 April, thank you. I hope all is fine with you and family, not withstanding you going through a bit of trauma with the repairs on your foot and other bits.

I read of the things being caused by the retaining screws. I guess it's a difficult injury—the foot takes all the weight, they cut a hole in your heel. I imagine you will feel that for a while.

I did wonder how long it would be before you worked out a way to ride your machine, but take care. I'm aware Harley got a new motor (years ago); I always wondered why they did that instead of just upgrading the Evo motor.

What is the advantage of the 17-inch wheels over the 16 inch? Regarding Joe's '05 Deuce got 17-inch, I read

45

years ago, it was critical on the front, stability-wise—the smaller wheel on the front oscillates on some situations, though I've never heard it actually caused real problems. I always assume smaller wheels were brought into being for some better ground, handling, I would imagine the overhead cam motor would be ultra reliable. Does Harley still have that separate oil tank?

At odd times Glen Dhu sends me a letter; a recent one informs me he has inoperable cancer—his liver about gone, the doctors give him about 12 months, maybe more with some intensive chemotherapy. He appears to accept it all, I guess not much choice. He wrote to me from Tassie; he's seeing a few things while he can, quit his job and says he will spend all his dough while he lasts, that cancer certainly takes a lot out, and really not much one can do about it. I was at a loss for words really on what I could say.

Hey, Al, I don't know if you seen it as yet a magazine called *Take Five*. Till a month ago I never heard of it, but a couple of people I know told me that they had a big story about me. I got a copy of the article sent in to me.

They have laid a heap of murders on me and all sorts of things. I mention this only because your mum may get a bit upset if she sees it; it's all the usual bullshit, but quite ferocious actually, and the author hasn't let things like the truth hinder his imagination. This article was in the 16th March '05 edition.

You are not telling me nothing new—that women (some) are something else; I understand what you are saying. I suppose one of the reasons they easier (or appear easy) to crack on to now is you are probably a lot more refined in how you deal with them when you meet up with them, particularly in the initial stage, and of course you

46

know they recognize what they see: home, good prospects, and no doubt you're not in a hurry, so they do the rest.

I can understand why they pursue you; why they write to me is a puzzle. I often get them, even had some crazy fuck from Mulawa prison (I used to write to her in the past, she was doing a few years and got out, but lasted about three months). She started writing again; in her last letter she asked me to marry her. I haven't replied to her.

But every month someone new writes; latest one was from Texas. She tells me she's 25, white (I noticed all the Yankee sheilas always let me know they're "white,") a model and into bikes and invites me to ask her anything. I ought to ask her why, as she only knows me from a website and nothing nice about me on it. Where at least you know me—we're not strangers.

Anyway I suppose I should have kept all of those letters, but fuck them. I got my latest appeal—petition to courts for a review out to Bill and co. They make copies and put it in folders, etc.—file it with court (Supreme Court). I will ask Bill to pass a copy on to you or Mum— see what I am on about (same grounds I always used).

Anyway, Al, I see you going okay. Soon I guess all that repair work you doing, the front dental will be done and you are 100 percent again. I guess Hank still okay. So take care and thanks again. Best regards, Ivan 18/4/2003

LETTER NUMBER 16

One Page from Ivan at HRMU 9 Goulburn C.C. Goulburn 2580 9th July 2005

Hello Al,

Hopefully all is fine with you and family. I received your letter on the 7th with the four photographs, thank you very much.

You really got your gym set up, quite impressive. Of course you have to do a bit; just look at those that don't. You see it every day, people the same age as you, but they look ten years older. (I had no idea you're 46—I tend to remember people still looking like I last seen them.

Hey, on the visit thing, don't concern yourself about that—it's a real pain for visitors, and they make it worse as time goes by. It is not important for me and time goes by. It's not important for me and as you say there is no doubt about parole; that would stop it for sure.

As you know, I keep on appealing; the latest is filed and I've been writing to folks—people who have an interest in the justice system. I write how the judiciary has been doing me over and I'm a bit concerned it will occur again. I even sent on of those concerns to NSW attorney general.

A recent reply from his office hinted on the course they're going on to sink me again. They refer to the fact in a 474 appeal I have raised that there has to be new evidence not raised previously at trial and said I cannot, just keep on appealing. I think they will go the technical route to dismiss my appeal.

Anyway good to hear from you—you do sound a bit better. The ambience of your letter is calmer. You got that computer printer well and truly sorted out now, so take it easy, and look after the young bloke.

My regards to your mum. I'm doing my best.

Best regards, Ivan 9 July 05.

LETTER NUMBER 17

Two Pages from Ivan at HRMU 9 Goulburn C.C. Goulburn 2580 4th August 2005

Hello Al,

Good to hear from you and hope all is still fine with you and your family. Your letter was received on the 3rd, thank you.

Of course I'm not surprised at how well you look even at 46-plus; actually, if you did not mention your age, I would have thought you had sent in a very old photograph taken about 6 to 7 years ago. I'm aware of how old you are, but you do not look it in a lot of ways. You will find as you get older you will not likely run into health problems normally associated with people that age; as you know a fit 40+ who has spent a bit of time in the past (you're always into fitness) can out-power and out-train younger folk.

There is not much you can do about broken bones, etc.—accidents (your foot!) Happen, except you can handle it well and recover a hell of a lot quicker; the pain is there, but you can cop it.

Remember (Michael) had a heart attack simply through absolutely lack of exercise. Bill talked to his doctor; his veins were completely fucked. He was only 50. I hope Henry's still doing a bit as well! I realise he may have some old injury as well—crook back! But still has to have a bit of a program to suit, that Bobcat rollover would have loosened him up a bit (your other photograph dated 14/7/05). Difficult to tell in that photo, but he looks a few lbs. heavy—imagine it was a bit cool at that—lots of warm clothes on!

Though I have never seen your home, your mum had told me a few years ago you were doing a good job on it, and you know what you want and are doing it. That's your goal and have got it—a lot not do that and it's a good hard struggle later on. Some habits are good. I note you very aware of it, if you can feel good, generally, all is good around you. Hopefully your young bloke will pick up the fitness bug as well.

You are right that things are only designed for politicians, look after themselves. Those three that just left Carr and co, their payout each year will make you weep.

Yes, that fucken shit media, unbelievable and what fucks me, the prison authority does nothing. Here the pricks go to the media and do a job on me and Shirley—I'm not coping it sweet at all. I don't give a fuck if they whack me in that prison OBS unit. All it is, is to overcome the appeal I have before the Supreme Court.

George is George; he believes what those pricks say.

51

Anyway, Al, thanks again for the news on things. (Hope your mum is okay.) You going good 'cause you work at it, and I will not be surprised at what you do achieve.

I do my best but fighting the government is difficult as one puts health, life in jeopardy, but I would rather do that than lay down.

I hope I survive my latest act. So best regards, Ivan 4/Aug./05

LETTER NUMBER 18

HMRU 9 Goulburn C.C. Goulburn 2580 3rd October 2005

Hello Al,

I imagine you gingerly stepping about after your latest medical adventure. Your recent letter spoke of the procedures you would have to endure; hopefully the operation was a complete success. Must be difficult to stay focused on business (work) and most ordinary everyday things. Knowing that is ahead, I suppose you plan things to overcome it. We can only hope it is the last of the major reconstruction work.

Quite a tidy repair bill on the Harley, though a lot of it is on additional bits and pieces. It must whack out some horsepower now. In regards to your knee problems, as you may know that area is one that a lot of work has been carried out; no doubt they probably will fix the problem.

I'm quite aware I will never be allowed to overturn my convictions; there is far too many reputations on the line for me to be allowed to get up. But that will not stop; I will take it to the next stage for a review. A major concern is this place, as they openly make it difficult for me, my reply will be raised to them soon enough. Anyway fuck them. I will do my best while I can.

I see things still a bit tough on the price of fuel. I imagine the price of big vehicles falling a bit. Bill and Carolynn tell me they bought a Mazda 3 recently; I believe it was a vehicle for Carolynn, but I guess it will be the main unit.

So thanks, Al. Hopefully next time, your reconstruction days are about over, and you can return to normal things.

Hope Mum is well—you take care. Best regards, Ivan 3/Oct./2005.

LETTER NUMBER 19

Two Pages from Ivan at HRMU 9. Goulburn 2580 15th September 2005

Giddy Al,

Glad to hear from you—your letter was received the 12th, thank you. Bloody hell, I cannot believe the hassles you getting over dentistry procedure you are going through. Hopefully all was successful and you enjoy the prospect of eating normally again—once you get used to the new teeth.

I can remember a couple of bike shops in Campbelltown, the Honda one in particular and another one close by. They were closer to the city, not far from the police station, but I guess they gone now. Twenty machines in 3 weeks for you, sounds okay to me, actually quite a few. Hopefully Joe sees the light and realises his business is in good hands, whether he's there or not.

Had an interesting day today. The prison commissioner, Woodham, came around today, with a bunch of shifty-looking stooges in suits. Came into my quarters, front room (he generally does—to show me off!), but this time he has that prick "Clive Small" with him. I have no idea why Small would be accompanying Woodham on a prison tour. Small is not a police person now; he is some sort of consultant about police matters for the government. He looks fucked now, like he got HIV-AIDS—probably off that other arsehole Marsden. He still is a lying prick as well; hopefully my diagnosis of AIDS is correct.

I had complained to Woodham about ordinary pricks getting onto the media and putting shit on me. And as Woodham does not allow me to write to the media or to a friendly advocate, so my side can be told. I asked Woodham that it should be his duty of care, etc. He relied on this question that he sent my letter (a copy) to the attorney general for their advice. That was fair enough, but seeing as today here he is, bringing the arsehole that I am complaining about (Small) on tours, I suppose my complaint can go out the door.

I also asked Woodham when I am due to get an exit program from here. Woodham told me: When you stop appealing or protesting your innocence, then you can go. I told him I will be protesting my innocence till the day I die. Small had an arsehole look on his face at that. I am very suspicious at Small turning up here, no doubt more shit about to be put on me.

The fucken Supreme Court refuses to answer my letters on what documents of mine are being placed before the judge who is consulting my application. I fear another cover-up by the judiciary on my miscarriage of justice.

Anyway, Al, thanks again for the letter. My regards to your family—hopefully your bodywork will soon be operating perfectly in the near future.

So, Al, take it easy and best regards, Ivan 15 September 2005.

56

LETTER NUMBER 20

From HRMU Two Pages from Ivan to Al 1st October 2005

Giddy Al,

Good to hear from you again and those things are going reasonably well; hopefully all is fine with your family.

I see you fighting fit mainly, but some pain comes at times. The exercise may be the cause of it – a bit, but probably it's due to all those operations, etc., you had—you laid off training and your body couldn't shape up quick enough. If you had any real major problems, your body would let you know when you were putting stress on it. Look at those footballers—they're as fit as you can get yet occasionally—bang—they blow something out. Anyway it does appear all that effort and pain you went through worked—good choice.

I read the specs of your new bike that you thinking of getting, sounds very good and why not—a new machine with new ideas. You got a good price for your one.

I spent two cups of coffee the other day just looking at a '06 Heritage soft tail 9 full colour spread) in this magazine I had. I'm surprised they still use the wire wheels (they look really excellent).

Congratulations on your latest promotion with the Rebels, though it was unexpected.

I know what you mean—you are just quite happy to roll along, obviously.

The members of your chapter thought they needed someone who could lead them.

Rather unusual for a Rebel to leave, to join another club. What would be the attraction, especially considering it causes serious trouble? Whatever is done has to be done carefully—no group discussions, as that is where witnesses later came from.

I do not know how things are really out there business-wise, but I see the government is sticking to the ordinary folk. They give themselves a hefty pay increase with benefits while saying it is better if everyone else gets a lower rate of pay, and they encourage some companies to bring in overseas workers to work at low rates, which causes every man to get low rates and then we can't really afford to buy things. Hopefully you can get Joe's business back up.

I heard about the half million + tanks the government brought and I knew it was a mistake; the country does not need them. They may be a super tank, but I suppose Howard wants to please Bush—I see he was trying to get 4 to 5 of the C17 cargo planes as well. They are about as good as those tanks are, they make good decisions.

Anyway as you say it's getting worse—I'm quite aware they will not give me a go. I'm still awaiting word from the courts over my latest application. I would not be surprised if they have decided and have not informed me and are hoping I will just sit here and wait.

So I hope your mum is fine, and for sure you will overcome your hassles—so thanks again and stay careful, particularly with that ex-Rebel business.

Good luck to you and family. Best regards, Ivan 1/Oct./2005

LETTER NUMBER 21

HRMU 9 Final Solution Centre. Goulburn C.C.

Goulburn 2580 26th October 2005

G'day, Al,

I was not aware of that book *Shallow Graves*; one would imagine it would be fairly ordinary, particularly as so much shit been said about me in the past, one would think it would be rather boring as what else is new, but that gay police minister Scully came up with some new stuff during his "dog day" media conference, "specialist in animal cruelty." Fucken politicians—really cannot expect much, they have to lie like fuck to cover up things.

What about that media arsehole—Walker!—walked out of that movie *Wolf Creek* when the prick seen the ones who were paid to walk out to say it's too scary! Walker is saying how he is a sensitive bloke as well; I guess his boyfriend might be impressed.

Then to top it off, I see on TV the other day Aus. Story—that actor who is the star in that movie—telling his story. I noticed how he kept making out he's not a poof, but why was he doing it on TV? No one would have guessed otherwise. I can imagine the film is violent, but what film isn't? If they have got to use me or "bad Brad" to give it a bit of a kick, it must be a dud.

Bathurst was a bit of a fiasco for some of the drivers— couldn't believe some of the shit that went on. I cannot work out why they race at Surfers; it's basically impossible to overtake and all they do is wreck their vehicles. It would make a great bike race.

Best regards, Ivan 26/October/2005.

If you end up in hospital again, *The Da Vinci Code* is quite an intriguing read.

LETTER NUMBER 22

One Page from Ivan at HRMU Prison, Supplies of Fine and Free Electrical Appliances to Me

G'day Al,

It's really good to hear from you again. It does appear I can receive mail again and reply to it. Thank you for the 9th August letter received on 19 August 2005.

No doubt Joe realises that as well. Forty-seven is nothing and you already know that; another twenty will be easily obtainable for you because of that buzz you get in doing good, and people do appreciate it when they get guided right. Also having a real mad product to sell just makes it 100 percent better; the way things appear to be going that will insure that more will want a machine that will also put a bit of life back into them.

As usual I'm doing my best despite the restrictions imposed on me. Again I await a court decision on whether I will be permitted to pursue justice; considering how they dealt with a similar application last year on the same matter, one cannot be very optimistic at all.

And of course all the other shit, that TV application I had, that got some cunts going and caused me to dig my heels in; the screws came in and took it because some arsehole politician got frightened by the shit the media put out. I got it all back, which was the only thing that I was going to accept. At least I'm glad that it pissed off that John Laws—he raved on a bit that I had those items.

Then that recent TV show—it had previously been on paid TV. A bit disappointed in George suggesting that I confessed to Mum and I don't give a fuck if he wishes to big note himself and cons the pricks that produced the show with his lies about me, I didn't like that bit about Mum. They certainly come up with some new things to convince everyone that I am guilty.

Anyway, I still do what I have to, so thanks again, and am glad to hear from you again and you keep on going okay. (I noted on the news, some bloke was running amuck in your area, street—shoving people—three, I believe, and he gets about on a pushbike).

You take care, and my regards to your family.

Regards, Ivan 20/august/2006.

LETTER NUMBER 23

From HRMU Two Pages from Ivan to Al 28th May 2007

Hello Al,

I hope all is still fine with you and your family. Your letter from the 17/5 was received 26, thank you, and it's good to hear young Kane now has a bar-free view

I see all that shit about the "REBS" and the "Bandidos" in the news and mororny going on to the media that they will basically wipe out the clubs that noisy pipes business really sucks. I read what you say on how it's policed, bloody difficult. One would really have to look into the act to see if there is any legal loopholes in the legislation, perhaps in how they do the tests and the test equipment and qualifications of the tester—who knows, there may be something.

I see you have a big investment with your new Harley—quite a bit of serious work being put into it and some high horsepower; hopefully all the war shit will settle down so you can properly enjoy it. I reckon it would fuck up noise levels with those RTA tests.

Congratulations on the ten years with the club. I cannot imagine the clubs Australia-wide will really allow the government to shut them down. Though the government will try to fuck you all over by using the police to hassle you.

Our Rebel friend here is still in the Bronx part. I really admire his style going all the way when his mate set fire to the fucken place.

And that shit recently about Muslims, to then become terrorists, it was total rubbish. The government, that particular minister, he knows no one is going to check it out, and being the racist arsehole he is, he bullshits to the media. The Muslims in here are a fairly docile bunch (there is quite a few); they get shit put on them all the time by the screws, and the Muslims calmly go on their way, never do anything.

Anyway I still battle on the courts still fucking me, this place fucking me. I've long given up caring about a lot of things and am about ready to say fuck it altogether.

So thanks again, glad to hear your mum is okay, and hope all goes good for you. I see you aware of all your shit—stay well and hopefully your bikes on the road. Best regards, Ivan 28/May/2007.

LETTER NUMBER 24

Two Pages for Al from Ivan at HRMU 16th July 2007

Hello Alistair,

Giddy, it was good to hear from you and hopefully all is fine with you and your family. Your letter was received the 14th, thank you.

The photograph shows you looking really well; I don't think anyone would guess how old you are by looking at that photo. That's a good idea, that bottom end (hog crank and rods) has a bit of stylistic strategy and for sure it will attract some comment.

I see all that warring shit on the news—raids on bike clubs—more like harassment, I think. The shitheads play it up while they cover up how fucked everything else is; of course the war between individual clubs—especially the shooting stuff—that sort attracts a lot of attention as well.

Our Rebel friend is still parked in the Bronx section— shitty conditions, though our section is not comfortable,

66

either; at least he still pisses them off. Another cell fire a couple of weeks ago, no damage to him.

I see that Stan Z is now eating shit; he made his name slurring everyone via his radio show as he picked on individuals and bagged the fuck out of them. Most people have a contradictory character associated with themselves—a bit of show, a bit of shit. S Z was a full-on, first-class sycophantic prick. I see a lot of cunts are praising him, but I note they are all fucken journalists.

They have a lot of shit; I see it in the news—hi-tech shit that can unscramble phone conversations, text messages, the hidden meanings! Though this is mainly directed at terrorist shit.

I thought that the camera/computer gadget is pretty deadly—it scans the number plates as the traffic goes by on an instant it checks if it's registered/stolen (if reported stolen). And buzzes up if there is a problem—very technical, scary shit.

Often one sees and reads of cases that decades later it is discovered by DNA tests that some poor unfortunate was wrongly executed, hung, as was that case you seen. He probably protested his innocence till he was swinging. The DNA in my case was not mine—that is why they speak of there must have been another or other persons there with me. Once they went on that course, I was stuffed.

I read that May '07 edition of *Woman's Weekly* (no doubt your mum has seen it, maybe). I was sent a couple of copies; there was an article in it about the family, usual fucked shit as they make out there is a big row between the Warthog and others in the Milat family. If you see it, you will see why I pointed out that it's hard to guess your age from that photo, and then take a look at Dick's photo (he

67

and Ronda in it). Bloody hell, they must have caught him first thing in the morning after a hard, long party or something.

As usual the Warthog carries on. I guess George thought it was important. Get a load of his outfit and his things.

Anyway, Al, I still does my best, and I appreciate what some still turn up and say a few things for me. So take care of yourself and your family. My best to your mum and others.

Best regards and respect, Ivan 16/July/2007.

LETTER NUMBER 25

Two Pages for Al from Ivan at HRMU 8th October 2007

Giddy Al,

It was good to hear from you, and I hope that all is fine with you and your family.

Yes, I see all that shit on me and could not believe that minister going on national media to put all that shit on me. I had been asking in here about some reasonable requests and was told because I was asking they cannot do it, so I wrote to the minister and he told me (and everyone else as well) in effect that I can get stuffed and that all I will get is a white lady funeral.

Well, now that everybody in power has told me to get fucked, I cannot argue with them anymore and have said to myself why argue with them. I only get lies in return so I will see how long I can last without eating. I of course will not know if that prick will keep his word about the white lady funeral; hopefully the family will hold him up to it.

So I have my hassles and I see that you still get the business medical-wise, the dentist making a mint and some pain on you—hopefully it has gone now.

That was no good, pulling up with some damage whilst training; perhaps some overwork caused it. I haven't done any training for a while. We have nothing at all—even one or two of the items you have would be good in here.

So hopefully you're back in training; at least you don't get the usual hurts that laziness brings on, and you certainly look a lot fitter than most. I've been reading about that shit, the bikie club wars. The things the police say the bike clubs are doing. Well how much can one believe the police? It must be a pain to have that bike and to have it going so well, but cannot use it because of all the problems that are around with club members.

That's very bad news about how Joe's business is going; it is really crook and it is very good of you to front up with him. Hopefully others can do it as well. Of course the banks don't care; I hope Joe can survive all of this okay and has structured his business to get something, at least.

Our Rebel friend is okay, out of the Bronx section, at least, though that did not concern him much and the fire business has to be tested in court; really he has more chance of getting out into the main than me. Of course they hate him, but they are like that to us all.

Yes I saw that Belanglo forest program. What a show and they really laid it into me, of course. They made it like that to look as bad as it could be. And also blame me for others as well, and the Warthog also putting up his head again. There is not much I can do about them making such shows; I just keep on with my stand and if someone inquires about something, I answer it. Of course the police

70

never actually do anything. They tell a few lies to the media and then the media makes up the rest.

So thanks again, Al, for your news and thoughts. Give my regards to all, and how it ends up for me is up to them—I really don't give a shit anymore.

And hopefully all goes good with you and your family, so my best regards and respect to you, Ivan. 7/October/2007.

LETTER NUMBER 26

Two Pages for Al from Ivan at HRMU 31st October 2007

Hello Al,

Thank you for the mail and the three photographs.

Hey, I cannot believe how they carry on about me. I never seen that newspaper article—they refused to give us that particular paper, and I'm well aware that they involve me in to whatever shit they were on about, something about some shit getting smuggled out! So the prison authority to cover it all up a bit brings me into it. And belittles our genuine complaints about this place to change the real issues.

This place is run by Macquarie Street (Parliament House), and they use their pet journalists to put shit on us. These Macquarie Street pets simply print whatever they are told to, as they use me at every opportunity because I mainly am the only me everybody is aware of.

Our Rebel friend had the right idea at what to do about this place, and he is still onto them.

They're always fucking me over and around, and that gets me doing things that makes it worse for me health-wise—it's just as well I don't give a fuck once I start those things. At the moment things are fairly normal, as some sanity finally prevailed.

The Supreme Court is still fucking me about; I had one of the HRMU counsellors give them a ring about my application for an inquiry into my matter. This was yesterday, the 30th, and the court register says that they will let me know when my application is put before a judge for consideration. It was last July that the court register sent me a letter about the application and how it had been allocated to one of the judges for his consolidation. So what can I do when they do this to me—I'm in a dangerous dilemma, as I cannot accept what they are doing to me.

I've read a bit about that Hicks and it would not surprise me at all what may have happened to him in those Afghani caves; I believe he gets out of prison at the end of the year.

That arthritis is bad news, though there are some real good medications that remove the aches and pains completely. I've had stuffed knees for quite a while. X-rays and all that shit confirmed it. For a while it was really hurting, the pills (Voltaren) fixed that; I now only use it occasionally—mainly in real cold whether it kicks back in.

Really try and avoid that knee reconstruction business—it will lay you up too much. Plus again you go through all the hassles connected with it—far better to wait ten years "if you can" as by then they will have greatly improved their techniques and you can rely on a pill a day to stop the pain till you are ready.

73

I certainly appreciate your words and I will always do my best to overcome my convictions, and I never really give a fuck at what the media lies about me, as it is only what they will do.

So, Al, good luck and best regards and respect, Ivan 31/October/ 2007.

LETTER NUMBER 27

One Page to Al from Ivan at HRMU
7th November 2007

Giddy Al,

Glad to hear from you; your 1 November letter was delivered on the 6th, thank you.

I see on the news how it is out there, the politicians say how good it is and others say how crook it is; I think what you say that it's bloody crook is correct.

A new bike will take your mind away from it, as you sort it out to sort your needs. Of course I would imagine that you would say that a new '96 Stroker was disappointing and very soft in all areas and to make it a reasonable machine, a 103 Stroker kit and modify the fuel system and generally grunt it up all way round.

The Rebel I hardly see unless in a distance, always in their faces, and that's good but you know how it ends up, and of course—crash, in the slow lane—very stark, bleak, though really that is nothing.

Yes, while there is an opposition party at Macquarie Street, I will be held here, though for a few weeks recently I had psyched up that I would not be spending the next Christmas in here. Fortunately for me, my health at best. That has been removed as the fucken courts finally respond to my correspondence. I had it in my mind that the screws here had been withholding my mail to the Supreme Court. Of course that thought in my head was quite real, and I was then on automatic.

I see what you are saying about people—how some act, cannot accept the bad times, as they expect others to carry them, stay chilled and keep on being prepared.

I loved it when that arsehole Scully 9 (the police minister) got the arse—'course he's still there but everyone knows he tells lies. They all do, but he got caught out.

Anyway, Al, thanks for the mail. You stay chilled. Hopefully all your family are fine—your mum and young Jesse and others also.

My regards to all and to you, 7th November 2006.

LETTER NUMBER 28

One Page to Al by Ivan at HRMU 5th January 2008 "THE DARKSIDE"

Giddy Al,

It is good to hear from, and I hope that you and your family are well. Your letter in reality reflects the truth of how it is out there, particularly the economics; it is so dear to live a reasonable lifestyle.

I see the government did the usual firework show—that's okay for the kids, I suppose, but it's pretty fucken ordinary; it would be more of a fun night if they sectioned off part of Sydney and let everyone run about with paintball (skirmish) guns and have a ball.

I read that DNA hair test business. I suppose the tests may identify something but till they get a suspect to match it, it really means nothing. Of course I noticed in that story no one asked what the police is doing about it—to close up things. I won't be relying on the pricks.

Of course my battle to get justice is being severely hampered by the government. Take your pick between the

77

attorney general department (who controls the courts) and the prison department. I've been trying to get a reply from the courts for the last 6 to 7 months.

I complained to the usual bunch of cunts—still no good. Yesterday a couple of letters turned up (including yours): one from the Supreme Court register who assured me that they have not received any correspondence from me since late February (my application); they said nothing at all has been received. And the other letter was from the Woodham Prison commissioner—and he has said that all my mail to the courts and the ombudsman was sent out of prison, had all the dates, etc.

Well who the fuck am I supposed to believe—the cunts have had me in a corner in here for years, and still they poke me with pointy sticks to stop me from making enquiries to the courts. The prison doesn't want—they (Woodham) tell me this, and the fucken courts don't want to hear from me either. Well when you're fucked, you just have to do a bit more.

Our reb friend okay, in another part here—no see now. He certainly pisses them off, but so, Al thanks again, and my best wishes to all of your family and best regard and respect to you.

Do well, Ivan 5/ January/2008.

LETTER NUMBER 29

Two Pages to Al from Ivan at Darkside Goulburn C.C. 28th January 2008

Giddy Al,

I hope that all is fine with you and your family; thank you for the 20 January letter.

Good to know that at least you could get away for a while for a bit of a run to see folks from all over to forget about the ordinary problems for a while, and of course the three photographs of young Jess were quite remarkable.

The DNA of those strands of hair—whom it belongs to is a mystery, but we knew of it at the trial that it wasn't mine. The prosecution and judge said that it was from an accomplice of mine; there was no evidence of who this/those accomplices were, but that's how they got over the DNA of the strands of hair by saying that. Of course it's plain to think that Ms. Walters pulled the hair from whoever was assaulting/attacking/killing her. He told the

79

jury that all it meant was that I did not assault attack, kill Ms. Walters.

The Crown did not make up quite a story of others and was a first-class goose and had no idea he was dazzled by all the media attention, so he simply went along with the shit that the crown put forward.

You have seen most of the shit said about me, and it is always only about me—I did this or that, and at times they do refer to the case that the crown had put forward, and the media then refers to that fucking arsehole judge who said in his view it was inevitable that others were there. Yet not once have I ever seen the media ask the police who these others are and what is being done about it.

I'm trying to do something, but the courts—their representatives, the clerks, and registers—refuse to acknowledge my correspondence, so I keep on with it.

I'm quite aware of those paid type channels—Sky! etc., though I've never seen one—and the shit they put me on.

I note your reference to make an application visit; well of course that would be great, but really you will get a lot of run-around; they still refuse to let Dick in, and only about six months ago, they let Wal in. They don't ask me, I have no say about it; they just use a lot of shit and pass the buck on the real reasons.

I see in Sunday's *Herald* (the 27th) a picture of a bloke waist-deep in water in Alaska—ice, snow, etc. He's using a suction dredge to suck up the gold—even now they're still finding it after a couple of hundred years of looking, over a thousand dollars an ounce now.

80

So the place is the same, nothing has been fixed; our friend is okay, though I haven't seen him for a while. Every now and again someone usually, mostly sheilas, writes to me. I think the Internet sky channels get them going.

So thanks again, hope business picks up for you and Joe, my regards to your mum, and stay well. Regards to your mum and stay well, regards.

And respect, Ivan. 28/January/ 2008.

LETTER NUMBER 30

Two Pages to Al from Ivan at Darkside 16th February 2008

Giddy Al,

It was good to hear from you, your 7th February letter received the 15th—thank you very much.

I read of your effort to sort out that "visit form" thing; bloody hell you certainly racked up some miles and phone calls over it. I've never seen those forms and am not familiar with them, though a few people have spoken about similar experiences that you have received; especially when they say to the police that they don't think that I did any of it, police certainly get a bit shitty about it. And do give them the run around, no wonder then they think most of the police are fucken arseholes.

I appreciate your efforts; it must have been so annoying for you. Well eventually the paperwork ends up in here (I never see, I'm not involved in it). Though they might see; it's Sydney who decides. It is here who says whether it happens. So good luck and hopefully it's successful.

It's unreal at what they say, and I see that you refer to the sky channel and it had "Alex Gave the Police Backpacks." No, Al, Alex is 100 percent with me. I do not know if you are really aware of what happened, but this is a bit of the story. Joan (Alex's missus) assisted the police, and they offered her the reward money if she would cooperate,

So whatever they said she agreed. This is why Alex divorced her, though that was going to happen anyway; Joan had left him a couple of times before, years before my shit happened.

Joan's hooked up with one of Alex's workmates; he was always there and always with Joan. Alex would be down at the gun club or the range or wherever, and this bloke (I forgot his name) was always there. Alex knew this, though I don't think he realised what was happening.

I honestly believe the bloke never had a fuck in his whole life before he met Joan. Joan used to treat him like a piece of shit, but it didn't make any difference to him; they went everywhere together. So it was Joan that said I gave her some backpacks; once I was convicted, she put her hand up for the reward money and the police refused as her evidence was not that hot. But it seems she had a written offer of this money—my defence did not know of this deal with the police and Joan.

So she got some money—quite a sum, I believe. The police kept it quiet, as they didn't want it known that they offered it to her, so she and her boyfriend are still together (when I knew him in 1990, odd, he was only about 35-odd—some must have thought Joan okay). So, Al, that is what happened.

Of course the Warthog found out how ready the media were to pay money for him to say whatever that they

83

wanted said, so he did; he would have done it whether or not Marilyn was involved. He's just and always was just a mutt.

One thing I always wondered though was that Alex did nothing about that bloke; even when Alex and Joan went to Queensland, so did he.

So time is flying past—fuck, I cannot believe how quick it goes here. Already we looking at how February is about gone, and I'm still here waiting for these cunts at the Supreme Court.

Anyway I hope that your mum is going okay. I suppose Hank is getting a bit of rain up his way, and I hope young Kane is going okay. I see you'll be 49 very soon—well you find that you adjust. At least you won't have half the problems a lot of other blokes have health-wise, at least. Best regards to Joe our Reb friend is okay, though I haven't seen him for a while—different section.

Stay well, best regards and respect, Ivan 16 February 2008.

LETTER NUMBER 31

Two Pages to Al from Ivan at Darkside, Goulburn C.C. 26th March 2008

G'day Al,

I hope that all is still fine with you and your family. Thank you for the mail, I always appreciate it.

Yeah! Months and try again, they say—you can wonder what the fuck that shit means. That is the usual shit that they say to everyone that attempts to visit me. They have been knocking family, friends for over ten years with basically the same excuse. Thanks for trying.

You're right how the time goes; it certainly marches past, and of course in here it's not a big deal—we just get older. Out there you would notice it, at least mostly you have stayed in front, a few adventures and despite hitting 49 you look as if you can handle whatever comes your way.

You have done well with young Jess going to school and getting into the shit that they teach you is terrific for him; hopefully he keeps at it for a while (I hated fucken school myself, but at least I learnt a few things there).

I see all that shit on the news—house prices going up then down, interest rates killing a lot, makes people lose their homes, repossessed, sold cheap. That was a good move you did to grab your house when you did. It makes a great difference to own it outright.

It has been in the news also again that the politicians want to get together—Australia-wide—to control bike gangs. Fuck, why pick on them! It may sound good to some cunts, but if it's simply outlawing bike clubs, it makes it easier then for you. You just ride around like everyone else does.

Your recent Newcastle run sounded good; hopefully you do a lot more. The Reb here going OK. I don't see him; he's in another section.

For sure the pricks won't be testing that hair by themselves. They know it's not mine that come out at the trial—the pricks tried to say it was from the girl (the victim) but, no, it's from someone, not from her—she pulled it out of the head from whom was attacking her.

I am aware of that copper (Adam Brooks), the leather jacket plus other stuff committed suicide (I heard his old man was a copper as well), so no wonder it got covered up so well. The government of course doesn't give a fuck as long as they got me. That's it.
You see how he had his son cremated so they couldn't do a DNA on his body, and he was suspected for the Bulli rapist and a suspect for the Balanglo murders. And his girlfriend Debbie tried to tell the police how he gave her the jacket from the German bloke and the watch that was

86

supposed to belong to the German girl—that was covered up, too. Nothing said again.

So anyway, I still battle on with it and they know it. Hope your mum is okay. My regards to all, best regard and much respect to you, 26/March/2008.

LETTER NUMBER 32

Two Pages to Al from Ivan at Darkside, Goulburn C.C. 22nd April 2008

Hello Al,

Greetings, I hope that this letter finds you and your family in high spirits. Thank you for the 11 April mail; I read your comments on the state of the economy and how business and most things is going downhill.

I see all this on the news, though not as you do—you're right in amongst it all and see it firsthand in that how it is hitting everyone. Joe's business was hit hard and that fucks a lot of people who rely on it—good to know it is still battling on slowly, perhaps.

I see the shit they put on the news; the government is going to do this or that and will sort it all out. Fucken pie-eyed plans and media falls over themselves to report it— you say like America! More like Zimbabwe, though not quite as bad as yet. I wonder who will be left to pay the bills, as all I mainly see on the news is shit about repossessions or big money-dealing business going under. Anyone who is evading tax, probably because they can't afford it.

I'm quite amazed at how the price of fuel is worldwide, actually. I seen on the news the other control, in the USA, some sheilas was whining because it now costs $50 to fill her car up—I think it's three times that here.

Of course it's possible they may listen in on the phones. I cannot concern myself; at my trial the pricks told the judge they had 4,200 hours of phone taps on me. The judge said to pick out the important bits for him to listen to, and they said they had none. For sure they will not chase up any leads.

I can imagine now they have done DNA on that hair (I think it was done years ago, though they don't say it); they have the compulsory DNA (taking DNA of prisoners) here—been in since 2000 odd, some mouth-swab shit. I refuse because they are pricks so they take it by force, hold you and pull hairs out of your arms, took a fucken heap. That was seven-odd years ago—no unsolved crimes connected to me through DNA. The point is they can do and do DNA from hair. That's why at the trial they came up with all that shit of another or another persons were involved as well because of those hairs in MS. Clark's hand and the vaginal swabs—it could all come from whoever attacked, murdered them. You see, they didn't follow that up either—whose hair is it (the copper's son who shot himself, so they say!).

I'm still doing everything I can, but the pricks at the Supreme Court ignore me. I will have to do more, eventually; I wonder at what some people think—they buy fucken homes at totally outrageous prices and then are fucked a few years on, through high interest, or they lose

89

their jobs or fuel is too dear. I was like you—I had no intention of paying off a house again. I just whacked it away and paid for the last one outright. Of course we know what happened, but getting framed up was the last thing I never counted on.

So thanks again, my regards to your mum. You stay well and also your family.

Best regards, respect always, Ivan 22/ April/2008.

Haven't seen the Reb for a while but hear he's OK.

LETTER NUMBER 33

Two Pages to Al from Ivan at Darkside Goulburn C.C.

Alistair,

Hello, good to hear from you. Your May letter was received the 9th—thank you very much; I hope that all is fine with you and family.

Yeah, we can be fairly certain that they do look at our mail very closely; it keeps them in a job.

As you say the economy does appear to be in difficulties, I see it in the news and at the moment it does not affect me very much at all in here, but it sure does impact on most of the people out there who rely on the everyday ordinary things. Anyone who thinks it will come good real soon will be mistaken, as you say, it isn't going to happen. I just sit back here and watch it, and it doesn't surprise me at all. I watched the government get big business—fuck them and the government sitting back waiting for it to come good. If it does happen, it won't happen for a while, and a lot more pain to come yet. You can wonder at the things that go on and why no one seen it

91

coming. Perhaps one day you may have to go bush living—solar, wind power, etc.

If things get really bad and certainly looks as if it will, not tomorrow or the next but it will come soon enough, hopefully it's far away, but I look at the way food is going—the price of it and the fuel is seemly just going way out of sight. In the old days it was the odd little war—terrorists, etc.—that caused a bit of a hiccup; prices went up but it always settled down and prices went down. Now they just go up, and big business is doing it.

I see in the news a lot of people losing homes as they bought at ridiculous prices and now the interest rises, food, fuel, everyday living has fucked them, and some smarty sells them out for a lot less than they paid. I imagine that there are a lot of nice rides going fairly cheap out there now; the worse thing is they may be cheap, but to run them is something else.

I note your $185 to fill your wagon—fucken hell! Imagine doing that each week, it sure takes a chunk out of one's wage.

And of course the government will be chasing more cash and use every way that they can; the tax people are always bad news and, as you say, some cunt is always willing to dog on someone.

Even in here we notice the price of things going up, Fucken rice used to be $2.10 for a kg; now it's $4.08 a kg. I don't buy the stuff but a lot of the lads do, and we are restricted to 2kg a buy-up.

I see on the news the squads went raiding at Park Lea and took the TV mob with them; weird shit that, I suppose, it makes the police feel safer. They even poke some gadget

92

down the shithouse to see what's down there amongst the turds.

That was a good ride you and the boys had to the city, only a few vehicles on the road, and a couple of homeless skanks to fuck. It sounds all right.

I've heard of similar shit. Over those phone taps, the cops say that secret codes are being used on covering up drug deals (e.g., the star stickers you had were called ecstasy tabs and fish was a code for drugs, etc.) And they keep on saying it with such authority that everyone accepts it, as I see you said they made you show them the stars stickers to clear it up, and well you got the fish from your friend who imported it, so they had nothing.

For the most part the public only hears one side of the story. I was never concerned over the jail DNA test thing; I just baulked at it to stuff them around a bit.

(I noted at that time in early 2000 every time it was raised on the news, they said it will clear up a lot of the old crimes and then show my picture on the TV; we are eight-odd years later, and no one has ever came in and asked me of old crimes to connect me with via DNA.)

Anyway I still battle on; hopefully Bill comes in this weekend. I made up a new court submission of new grounds of evidence; I don't send it by mail, as the pricks at the court say they don't receive it. Bill and Carolynn are off again, another field trip— Darwin this time. They really get into this travelling over the place, just finished an 89-day trip about three weeks ago. They got one of those mobile home things—doesn't look too bad and is fairly cheap to run: 12 litres to 100km. Bill says weighs 4-and-a-half tonnes. Bill if he gets in will file my shit with the court. It will piss the court and government off a bit again.

93

I haven't seen the Reb for a while—another section than me, but heard he's going okay, always does.

So, Al, thanks again. You stay well and your family as well. Best respect and regards,

Ivan 11/May/2008.

LETTER NUMBER 34

Two Pages to Al from Ivan at Darkside Goulburn C.C. 29th June 2008

Giddy Al,

Hello, I was glad to hear from you and hope that this letter is received by you in very good health and that all is fine with your family.

Yes, it is very cold down here now; one has to keep rugged up, otherwise pneumonia or some other shit has fucked one up completely, and of course it plays havoc with one's arthritis.

So I see it is getting worse every week out there for all you folk; it's all I see on the news. People losing their homes, getting their vehicles repossessed, fuel prices rising every two to three days, and traffic gets fucked every second day or so because something fucks up. At least a couple of you can recognise it.

I love watching the politicians as they talk about it all; the ones who are responsible for all the fuckups say that they will look into it, and the opposition party tells us how stupid those incompetent pricks are and say some shit that an inquiry should be held into it and then because the government is in the shit again. They wheel out some arsehole like Campbell (police minister) who gets on the news saying how successful the gang crackdown is going and there has been 500-plus charges laid upon bikie gangs (outlaw ones) because of Operation Ramado (some name like that), or the prison minister will get a press conference up that he is passing laws to keep dangerous prisoners in prison for longer or make it impossible for them to get released. Of course the whole state is going belly up; they cannot help their buses on the road. I hear all the shit in the news.

Yes I did see another show on TV a few weeks ago: *Crimes That Shocked the World— Backpack Killer*—never seen that one before. Rather stupid, I thought—of course it makes me as guilty as hell. I notice there are a lot of reruns on that show lately.

The courts received my latest submissions for a review—they notified me of that, I gave them to Bill and he put them in or otherwise the cunts deny getting them if I send them in. Hopefully they do look at them instead of just sitting on them.

As you say, no one has seen all the shit coming, the house loans business—they seem to blame the Yanks for it, the fuel appears to be a worldwide thing and nothing no government can appear to fix, though a lot of cunts are worrying a hell of a lot about whales—they cannot save them fuckers either because the Japs like eating them.

It may be that some foreign pricks are causing a lot of this, fuel prices, etc.; it certainly has put a big break on things. See Joe still hanging in—that's good and he may survive it okay. Really I suppose all he can do is keep on going for as long as he can, but it does seem to be a real uphill battle despite his best efforts. I hope that he keeps some of his emergency fund to save himself, no sense in going under altogether. You will have to keep a sharp eye out on it that Joe's business being tied up in your bike; I imagine you are aware of it.

Shappelle Corby—a couple of stories on her lately. I cannot see how anybody can believe someone who is paid to tell a story a certain way. The media loves to jump on some poor cunt, and they really crucify people at times.

So anyway, I'm glad to see you taking care of yourself okay. As you know, it won't be easy as time goes on and no one can really afford a lot of things that one took for granted. Hopefully you are ready if it ever gets that bad.

Well not much happening in here—cold, yes, it always is in winter. As far as I know, our Rebel is okay. That fire matter goes to court early November—should be an interesting case. I hope your mum is going okay (hope she's keeping rugged up as well) and young Jess as well. So thanks again, Al. You take care. My best regards, Ivan 26/June/2008.

LETTER NUMBER 35

One Page to Al from Ivan at Darkside Goulburn C.C. 23rd August 2008

Hello Alistair,

Thank you for the 18th August letter received the 22nd. Joe seems to be stuck in his own ways with the shop and he doesn't change, always in the red; maybe you can help him so he can move forward. With your knowledge on motorbikes, and you seem to know everybody in the bike world so you would attract business, I'm sure the two of you will get it going again.

Well I see your assessment on how Joe's motorbike shop is going—rather unfortunate, of course, as it does seem he is on very shaky ground for himself and some others; hopefully you are able to retain it.

This was a fucked thing, the four bandits jumping one of your lads. Of course it creates more trouble. I can see it getting really nasty, so be ready.

Well no one ever knows how important it is to look after one's health for when one gets on a bit; in the old days people just died because the doctors couldn't fix them. Now they can really work a bit of magic on people.

I must say, you in particular have had some major reconstruction done on you on various things, ankle, shoulder, so as long as they can do it, it would be worth living if one never took a few bruises, so to speak, in one's life travels. They will fix the pain up in no time or you will accept it as part of you—I'm in this position.

That's for sure a Rudd won't turn things around, no one can for a while, and they keep going on that the Chinese will keep us going, Well all that is they will pay the government's bills and a lot of the country will go down the gurgler. I laugh at our premier; he wants to sell everything—to pay what. I see the prison guards got over 40 million dollars on overtime alone this financial year; it will be more next year.

The Supreme Court fucked me over, simply altered a few facts. And dismissed my application. So bad times ahead for me now. I never expected too much but not so blatant lies like that.

I hope Dick going along okay and his family.

So thanks again, Al. Hopefully all will be fine with you real soon. I hope your mum is fine. You be careful with your health—the docs do know a bit.

My best regards and much respect, Ivan 23 August 2008.

LETTER NUMBER 36

Two Pages to Al from Ivan at Darkside Goulburn C.C. 20th November 2008

Hello Alistair,

G'day and thank you for your 16/11 mail, received the 20th, and may all be well with you and your family.

Yes, that Rudd money coming in December will certainly make a lot of needy folk a lot more comfortable over the oncoming Christmas, and as you say it is about time the government did something for the people who had been screwed for years, so now a lot of people who have been battling lately can face X-mas with a lot more confidence. That Rudd is a pretty smart dude when he is forced into a corner as he is now.

Well for a while now you have been saying about the boom and good, easy times were coming to an end, while other pricks were saying it will be okay, it's going to get better. Your prophesy has come true, as every country in the world has had their economics turned upside-down, and as you say it will get a bit more worse yet; we can see how desperate it is as the governments throughout the world pump untold billions of dollars into schemes to rescue themselves.

The only business that is picking up is the piracy business—them Somalian lads certainly are increasing their cash flow, grabbing that big Saudi tanker and other cargo vessels is really pissing some governments off.

I see all this shit in the news, but one can hardly believe what the media tells us or any of those government cunts. I'm finding your accounts of how it is out there to be more incredible.

Nothing will really affect us in here, as we get fuck all anyway. I had a bit of a laugh at the NSW premier budget a couple of weeks ago. His government is obviously running out of cash to pay its own bills, and his solution is to jack up some tolls in peak hours and of course the poor old motorists, some of them cannot avoid the extra charges and I think that he will sell off a bit more of the government departments. The prison department is stuffing him about but as they require a lot have overtime to run this place.

Anyway its good news to hear Joe is still trading okay, as that means you are still going okay.

I often see on the news the troubles amongst the different clubs, and it's seemly Australia-wide as people get whacked by unknown assailants, and they are all involved in some way in a bikie club.

I haven't seen the Reb for a while, as he is in another section; their trial was supposed to start earlier this month, the setting-fire-to-the-prison business. This place is getting me down—I'm about ready to say fuck it and get put into a little room and get drugged up so I don't have to get involved with arrogant arseholes and ridiculous rules.

I had a friend go into the Sydney office of the High Court to file for me an application to appeal. The pricks at the High Court refused to take it because it was handwritten (we don't have access to computers, typing, printers, etc., anymore), so I wrote it by hand, the High Court doesn't like it but, so once I found out this, I raised it here with the prison management and so they typed up my shit for me (I paid for the photocopying—384 pages at 50 cents a page). I was a bit surprised that prison management did the typing; I had expected I was going to have a painful argument with the High Court over this. So I sent off the typed-up shit and hopefully my Sydney friend will get it and put it to the High Court.

So again thanks, Al, say g'day to your mum for me. You stay well and my best regards and respect, Ivan
20/November/2008.

You know you could write a real good book based on your life and what goes on—you ought to think about it.

LETTER NUMBER 37

Two Pages to Al from Ivan at Darkside Goulburn C.C. 10th December 2008

Hey Alistair,

G'day, I hope that all is fine with you and family, and thank you for the mail 1st Dec. received on the 8th.

Well I'm glad you received some of that Rudd government bonus money, it certainly is getting some attention from a lot of so-called experts. The folks that are getting that cash are the disadvantaged in that they mainly live on a daily/weekly basis on a minimal amount, and to get this extra will certainly make it a bit more comfortable as now they can have some real cash in their pockets to do with it as they please.

Our countries are seemingly giving the money to a lot of big companies to get them out of the shit; at least Rudd and Co are spreading it around. I think he is doing okay in what he is doing—no sense in the government keeping it for later. As you say, people out there are finding it tough and for everyone that is working, and now Rudd has made their life a bit better.

Unless the other big countries pick up, Australia cannot pick up, as it relies on them to buy our mineral products, ore, etc., and everything I see on the news (another country goes into recession)—no one making anything because no one's buying.

At least those little Somalians are having a go, grabbing that tanker and other ships; that will bring in a few dollars for them. It's a desperate country, and what else can they do? They have no fear, as if they do nothing they are fucked and so are their families. At least now they can provide something for them.

I read all that shit about prison overcrowding and no funds because the screws get all of it in overtime and yet they arrest anyone for anything.

The lebs are certainly in the news lately, and of course because they have made some of them look like dopes and they put shit on everyone when they finally catch them out. And that is exactly how it is—there is no respect anywhere, and they never take the time to listen and rely on the fact that because there is 5 or 6 onto one, so they must be right.

I don't give a fuck anymore. I just roll along and if they want to be arseholes, fair enough, so I will be, too. I've got nothing to lose, only this place, and it really sounds like a good idea at the moment.

I wonder why all those easy riders decide to join the Rebels like that, perhaps for the prestige? It has to benefit your club—the extra fees, etc.

104

So thanks again, Al. May you and family have a good X-mas. My regards to Henry and co. Stay well and best regards, respect, Ivan 10/December/2008.

LETTER NUMBER 38

Two Pages 4th February 2009

Hello Alistair,

Good to hear from you. Your 24 January letter was received on the 2 Feb., thank you very much.

Due to that business over my hand, (finger cut off) it was not till the 2 Feb. before I was able to get anything or even see daylight, so to speak, and even now they are imposing a lot more restrictions upon me.

So I read your letter about things out there and I see the news, which reflects what you say that things are really crook out there; it does appear that things are really crook out there. It does appear some people are going okay and these government handouts are a bit of a bonus—if get it. I see on the news that the opposition will block the package in Parliament.

But as you know (and say), things are going good and the government is pumping money into the system; eventually it will slowly grind to a halt unless something dramatic can be done to come up with a solution.

I note that you mention that you can ride about into town, etc., because things have been resolved; hopefully it is so, though I see on the news today, the Hell's Angels outfit was blown up and shot up, by some unknown persons. Of course it could be anyone, an internal dispute, personal grudge, etc., but, Al, take a bit of care out there. I am sure that you are very aware of what is going on.

Yes, it does seem at times that the police now are solving a few old serious crimes—a big deal was made up by the media a couple of weeks ago of it. Whether it was technology that made the initial breakthrough in that case is unknown. I seem to think it would be more likely someone got caught on some matters and to get out of it, and then the technology came into it—phone taps, bugs, wired up, mutts—and then they lowered the net over them. You can bet money that most bent coppers will be secretly bugging other crook cops, politicians, etc., to cover their own arses to stuff others up and then all comes undone.

I only heard a while back that John Preston passed away, probably a heart attack?
He was a few years younger than me, but never stayed on top of himself.

I find it extremely difficult to get motivated health-wise and now, particularly with this business and how the prison keepers are carrying on about it by taking stuff off me, it only exacerbates my health further in decline and, worse, I don't care how bad it gets. Also today I got a letter from your mum. I will write a reply over the weekend, as I cannot get more envelopes till Friday.

I had my good reasons to do what I did. The High Court has said that I could file for a special leave to appeal application against the 17th of July 2008 decision of the

107

Supreme Court, and tells me that only if I comply with all the High Court rules, paperwork, typed up, copies, time limits, etc. So what is my chances in here, I've argued. Written letters, you name it—I've done it and all just to appeal. The High Court doesn't want to hear my difficulties and stopped replying, so what was left.

Your mum said some media attention was raised over why I did it and a lot of people are giving their answers. I've seen none of it; they had me buried out of the way. I hardly knew what day it was when they let me out, so now I am more isolated than before. But that has been my lot since 1998, so nothing new there.

Anyway, Al, thanks again. I appreciate your thoughts and time. I want to buy one of those little write type-up machines but they won't let me, so I battle on with my pen.

You take care, my regards to your mum and co.

Regards and respect, Ivan 4 /Feb./2009.

LETTER NUMBER 39

From the Bronx, Goulburn C.C. 21st February 2009

Hello Alistair,

And hi, thank you for the 16 Feb. letter received the 19th. I think everyone's eyes get a bit crook as they hit fifty; I had to get reading glasses then as well.

I see that they did catch one bloke in Victoria for some of those fires, but they reckon he needs psychiatric care. I can imagine the cops interviewed him.

I never cut my finger off to go anywhere; I was surprised at them wheeling me into that hospital. It was my way to say how fucked the court system is. I've been told a lot of people had a lot to say about why I did it; I didn't see or hear any of that shit—they had me well and truly out of the way, and I didn't see sunlight for a week later.

Since then the prison management is really giving me the business: no razors, no prison issue plates, no knives to cut up food, so I've hardly eaten much since that finger business and since they are trying to fuck me up.

I'll do it myself and rather starve than be forced to rip up my food with my hands.

I have sufficient funds to buy a type/printer, copier machine, but they won't let me purchase one, and I am certainly not going to sit around here if I can't appeal my case to the courts. I would rather starve myself in front of them first.

I think it may be risky as a rise in interest rates will cause panic, even a small rise will cause panic, as I see it a lot of people have bought new homes because the government gave them all that money to get started, and now all they have to do is pay it off for the next twenty-five years—as long as they have a job it will be okay, but it better be a secure job, a government one, at least. All I see on the news is gloom; all the car companies seem to be going down the gurgler, and every government is simply giving away all their money. Crazy times, all right.

I watched with interest all that shit that went on about the bush fires; they were interviewing everyone, even gave close-ups of koala bears. Someone is going to be rich out of that money that was handed over.

Best regards and respect, Ivan 21 /Feb/2009.

LETTER NUMBER 40

One Page to Al from Ivan at Darkside Goulburn C.C. 23rd March 2009

Hello Alistair,

Yes, that's all I see and hear on the news—now is the doom/gloom, and it's going to get worse. It certainly appears to be rushing headlong into harder times, and none of those shitty politicians will be able to change it, though each will make up grand schemes.

And what about that ex-judge, 3 years for lying—a bit mad, not that I give a fuck as to what they do to him. He ought to kick his defence team up the arse. Though, once he confessed he was well and truly fucked, and then after confessing they wheel all those pricks in to say what a great chap he has been—what a fucken defence plan. On appeal he will get a non-custodial sentence, though.

I see three of your club members died: one shot, one was drunk and fell asleep and choked on his spew, and the other died from a blood clot to the brain. And rather sad the three funerals—getting shot is difficult to dodge, especially if you are not really expecting it and or would think it

111

won't happen to me. Getting pissed and then choke on own spew—at least he must have been having a great time and never really realised what was happening.

Heart attacks seemingly happen quite unexpectedly, though the unfit ones are always a candidate as like any if it's not looked after, whether is a motor or yourself, it will fuck up and break down, and a lot do not really take care of themselves. I have no doubt that you can easily pass for a 40-year-old. You certainly don't look fifty—good choice you made to take care of yourself a bit (health-wise) and the other wise moves. Think ahead a bit and it doesn't really matter about others letting you down. You get Jess and you going okay, while others wonder what went wrong.

Things are real shit in here. I get a lot of attitude and nothing else, so I simply shut down and say fuck it, I'm getting nothing, but I refuse to cringe like a dog whinging about it. I realise it was hopeless saying anything as to how I feel about things, as they like to hear that one is suffering over what they do. It's a downhill road, but inner peace sets in after 3 to 4 days and no one loses any concerns as I realise I am only losing all this shit that they seemly keep putting on me.

So thanks again, Al. Keep yourself aware—my best regards to family, your mum. Stay in luck and health.

Regards and respect, Ivan. 23/3/09.

LETTER NUMBER 41

One Page to Al from Ivan at Darkside Goulburn C.C. 23rd April 2009

G'day Alistair,

And may all be fine with you and your family—thank you for the 12 April mail received the 20th.

Yes, I have watched all the attention that has been put on the bikie gangs-clubs; for a while it was the main point of the news, and some of the shit said about it all sounded real good. Whether it is true is another story, but as you say they are really making it quite difficult for the club members to meet.

It's so easy for the police to pick up anyone and say he had a gun or drugs on him—a pity that it may get closed down as no one is going to keep on going knowing the police will keep on hassling them.

No doubt someone will come up with something else, though it will never be the same as it was.

As you know, the NSW government is really in the shit—power goes out, trains are crook, roads jammed, schools are fucked, so it was easy to pass a few laws and blame it on biker gangs.

Yes, that dopey ex-judge and his defence, yes, should have went to the mental way, but fuck the arsehole anyway—at least now they can never use him again.

Fifty is okay, especially when you don't look it, and you don't and mainly stayed ahead of things and do better than most. I see it is getting worse every day. That's tough that Joe has to do that, sell that place—Billy is going into a townhouse, hopefully something does turn up for them.

Things here are still the same; they are kidding themselves if they think I am just going to sit in here like a silly cunt.

I'll have to send Woodham something next time, I think. I'm out of the Bronx, not that there is much difference, really—a bit more room, but I never give a shit about that and really when it comes down to it, why give a shit about anything. So things have to change a bit or I will be back in the fucken headlines again.

So, Al, you're doing okay, so keep doing what you do best and what you think is best.

Thanks again for the mail. Always glad to hear the truth of how it is out there.

Best regards and respect, Ivan 23 April 2009.

114

LETTER NUMBER 42

Two Pages to Al from Ivan at Darkside Goulburn C.C. 10th May 2009

Hello Alistair,

G'day good to hear from you. Thank you for the mail (29th April) and three photographs received on 6th May.

Well it's unfortunate you had to leave the club particularly because the government has decided to force the club, its members to break up or get arrested. So considering what can happen, you probably did make a wise choice. The ones (different clubs) that have been arrested appear to find it very difficult to get bail, as most are alleged to have weapons, drugs and other things illegal in their possession, or allegations of violence, etc.

I see all the shit on the news even film of a heap of riders in Adelaide; well each have to decide on how they react to this bit of government bastardry. Maybe something may have come out of that Adelaide meeting, because spending a lot of money on a show of solidarity? Like that

115

the media mutts attempt to suggest it was a show of force. Of course in time, there will be ways to circumvent the current legislation. That Adelaide money might have been better spent on briefing a lawyer to study it. But as you say, it's a bit silly to keep turning up to the club and get arrested and probably fitted up with dodgy allegations. And no bail and lose a lot of things—it was a wise choice, Al.

No, I am still in what is called "Super Max" (Dark side). They had shot me into the "Bronx." Over that finger-off business. The Bronx is the shittier section of what is a shit place, mainly smaller area to move and in my case total solitude. I didn't give a shit either way, as all it did to me was to consider re-splitting my hand open and pulling some parts out and perhaps putting that in the mail to some arsehole. I am close to doing that on a couple of occasions. Then they moved me back to the ordinary Dark side section—a bit more room, see others, etc.

But things are still the same with me as it was on 26th Jan 09. (Cut that finger off to highlight the situation I have with the courts.)

Well the courts still telling me to piss off and I have sat in here for seven-and-a-half years and nothing to do. Prison management doesn't cater to one's mind or spirit in here—nothing in here to keep one's mind-spirit intact, so I've asked for things (at my cost, I pay for it) but they say no, so fuck it. I've decided it's not worth it to keep arguing and have stopped eating from this weekend; of course I will keep trying to get some response from the courts and try and get management here to do a bit more. I am not actually telling them what I am doing, as I am simply fucked and not going to argue the point.

Our reb friend and his mate did well in court not so long ago. Due to a massive change of mind by management

116

here in darkside. They burn everything in their room area $30.000 damage bill and charged. But their defence was going to be that the system in here causes us to do extraordinary acts, so we were to be subpoenaed to tell of this place; its' like Guantanamo Bay—the protocols used. Anyway the ABC (channels 1 and 2) got permission to film the proceedings, but on the second day the D.P.P, corrective services, pulled the pin, dropped the charges, so it's done and dusted—no penalty to the boys. It would have been a hoot of a show if it did proceed.

That's all I see on the news: people losing jobs, the government saying it's not so bad now but will get worse. The news is, as you say, there's a lot going down the gurgler. And it does seem that Joe is really trying to stay on top of his difficulties selling more assets; if that does not work, everything is lost. You can see that problem that everything is stuffed and it will get worse yet. It's unfortunate how it's going. Of course you could have quite a harem and no doubt they will put it on you, so good luck on how you handle it.

So anyway who knows how it will go; it certainly looks crook all over. At least you're keeping on top, and I'm glad to hear your mum is going okay. So my regards to all.

You be careful as usual on all things. My thanks again with best regards and respect from me, Ivan. 10/May/2009.

LETTER NUMBER 43

One Page to Al by Ivan at Darkside Goulburn C.C.

G'day Alistair,

Yes, it is bloody cold up in here. Thank you for the mail of 26th June, received 2nd July.

I am glad that Bill put that letter to Woman's Weekly; as you know the media crucified me with their lies about that finger business. Perhaps at least people can see the real story; hopefully *Woman's Weekly* printed it all. A lot of shit gets put out on me, especially on that website thing, and I'm told a lot of people do look at all that shit on the Net/Web.

In here they use what's called the safe cell to break you down.
It's a total enclosed cement box, a lot smaller than an ordinary cell, no openings of any kind, nothing in it, cannot tell whether it's day or night, cannot hear anything. I refuse to eat so after a couple of days of it, I don't give a fuck.

I see the police still going on about the bikie brawl at the airport, arresting more over the last few days. Fuck, you would think by now that anyone who was involved would have left the state for a while instead of hanging around at home.

I doubt if the governments would say anything if a giant meteorite was going to smack into the Earth, but it would get a lot of people praying if they knew it was coming. I seen that shit in Parliament—it goes on a lot.

Anyway, Al, I'm still doing my bit to keep the pricks going. The court's still fucking about, and I'm hassling the prison minister about this place, nothing to do.

Woodham sent me a real nasty letter a few days ago, like they fuck me completely and they wonder why I now don't give a rat's arse and am about ready to chew out another finger.

So thanks again, Al. My regards to all—you stay on top.

Regards, respect to you, Ivan. 4th/June/2009.

LETTER NUMBER 44

Two Pages to Al from Ivan at Darkside Goulburn C. C. 13th June 2009

G'day Alistair,

And about my letter or parts of it being in the woman's weekly, to date I have not seen that article.

For seven days after I chopped my finger off, I was locked away (safe cell?) light on 20 hours a day, no idea of time. It's in a cement box, no windows or openings. The best way I deal with that shit is don't eat, and after a couple of days I had all that pain in my hand, so after a couple of days I didn't give a fuck what happened. It took seven days to negotiate as usual once I agreed to start eating.

I had no idea what was being said as to why I did chop my finger off, though the screws did say the media put a lot of shit on me. The first thing I did was write a letter to Bill and Carol, and explain exactly why I did it. I found out later that in that week when all that shit was being put on

120

me, that lady editor of woman's weekly rang up Bill and Carol about that finger business. So when that letter arrived at their place, they realised what my story was, and why I did such a thing—that it was either I do something or I give up because the government (the High Court) was being real arseholes.

So I choose my way, and I don't regret it at all and will do it again when meanness and unreasonableness is used against me.

I do not think that any money was involved; Bill and Carol are not like the WARTHOG. Whether *Woman's Weekly* has printed my reasons and not altered them, in time I will know as I've asked a person to send me that article.

I'm surprised it took *Woman's Weekly* such a long time to print up, as it was in early February they had the true facts. And if *Woman's Weekly* decided to write up a contrary story than mine, well so it be it—just shows what the media is.

I always appreciate it when family do things for me, to assist me, even when they get double-crossed, which mostly does occur because media government lies sound a much better story.

So thanks for your 5th of June letter received on the 10th; of course you must feel quite unwell in your heart after the loss of the club—a lot of good mates and now you can't say g'day without fear of arrest. And hell, there is nothing else so to speak going on to match what you had in the club. In the club everybody has the same interests, age did not matter; in ordinary life, an oldie can only hang out with other oldies, a bunch of old drunks—fuck that.

121

I see that it's getting worse for most out there; I see today one of the banks raised its rates for home loans because their profits were falling. I'm certainly glad at least the government got that cash out, that X-mas extra bit and whatever else, as I notice the price of oil is creeping up. So everything is on the up and up.

The politicians—who can you believe? I watch them on TV and question time/senate. They put shit on each other. I see what you say as to how Rudd is doing things, getting us in debt! Well at least he is doing something—that other bloke, except for raising the price of smokes as an answer, says they wouldn't do anything. Good luck and hopes! Perhaps at least it livens ups the place.

It certainly looks as if it is going down the gurgler; it may pick up a bit for a while, but unless most of the people can get back into making things, it won't last. And yes about 2012—it will really be tough.

The environment is going to pieces, the ice is slowly melting. Perhaps if more factories go bust, it may slow that meltdown. I see GM in the USA is arse up, so at least again less smoke heating the planet.

Yes, things are getting worse here. In here I'm concerned at what I will do next; after seven-and-a-half years sitting here with nothing to do has fucked me, I'm determined to either get something to do to keep me busy or next time I post bits of me to fucken Woodham. Whatever does occur, if they forced me into damaging myself, if I survive it, they will have to ship me out of this fuck-up place.

The only real thing keeping me going here is awaiting the High Court people, to decide on how I am to proceed with an appeal. If it's bad news, well, I'm fucked, so

122

nothing will matter. And it's easier then to do things to fuck them, so to speak, and give the media something else to write about.

Hope Joe going okay still, and Henry's fortunes and spirit goes better.

Thanks again, Al. My regards to your mum, my regards and respect to you, Ivan13/June/2009.

LETTER NUMBER 45

Two Pages to Al from Ivan at Darkside Goulburn C.C. 23rd July 2009

G'day Alistair,

Yes, even the weather is out of control here, mostly freezing. Winter in here, so the heating system often packs up and pumps cold air in, so one gets a touch of flu and generally feels fucked-up most times.

Yes, that safe cement box, often in here, they conduct tours of this place. A dozen or more gronks walk and see; I've seen a dozen or so of these gronks squeeze into the safe cell. It's a lot smaller than an ordinary prison cell; when they come out they all smile and nod at the screw who is leading this walk-and-see-shit tour. No one says, "What an inhuman place to lock someone in—no windows, no openings, a sealed cement box, continuous lights on, and no idea of sense of time."

I look at these gronk tourists and wonder what the fuck they are looking at. The gulag features us prisoners, the

124

screws tell them that me/us are the worst prisoners in the state, we have to be leg-shackled, handcuffed, even, to go 50 to 60 metres to visits or the medical clinic and escorted by 4 or 5 screws and this place is a building, a box in a box.

No wonder the gronks are impressed—they are told all this shit and it looks the part, especially as this place is promoted as the worst, hardest prison because the worst prisoners are in it.

For near on eight years, I've been hearing all this shit about me. I've had arsehole government ministers, the commissioner and other arseholes who want to get there name in the media, and they all put shit on me.

I just sit in here, yet all this shit put on me and then I am told, "Well, you got such a bad reputation, you have to stay here." The cunts are out of control—they tell so many lies about me, and they use their lies. I've told the ministers that I'm fucked and don't care, that "you do something or I will," so one morning I will wake up and say this is a good day to be an arsehole.

I just don't give a fuck anymore, and really hope that some prick stirs me up, particularly management.

So who knows how I will end up. Thanks a lot for the mail and the three photographs. Young Jess is really bulking up and powering on, but he's got a long way to catch up to you. You don't change much. I wish I had a bit of exercise gear here to keep me busy during the day; their idea of an exercise yard is a bare cement zoo-type cage out in the fucken cold. I never go there. One can get all sorts of issues that really fucks everything; in other words, it can take 20 to 30 years off your life and makes a misery as it occurs.

125

I hardly see any shit about bikies these days, as you say they have broken up the clubs with the threat of prison, but there will be the bike shops—everyone loves a Harley.

I see on the news the government saying how things are fucking up, shops doing good business go down the gurgler with only a few left, but everyone has to eat, buy shit to survive—clothes, etc., even those without jobs—so the fewer shops get their extra business. It will always be like that: a lot more goes down, less jobs, but everyone still needs stuff.

The government really does some spinning these days that has really picked up.

That's bad news about your mum. I was aware of the heart issue but only one kidney working and it's not going so good either. I see a lot of shit on the news about health, hospitals, fundings, cannot cope. Well it's always been like that, though it's getting a bit overwhelmed as more people are getting older, and problems arise.

I think my kidneys are okay. I am sure I have got a few urgent health issues that I would get looked at out there, but my kidneys I think are okay, and I would gladly give one up in its need.

There's a lot of islanders, lebs in here (prison generally). I hear they run all the rackets, mainly, the Asians took over from the Aussies, and the lebs/islanders now took over; they do get out of control a bit.

So, Al, I was glad to hear from you.
And my regards to all, best regards—respect to you, Ivan 27/3/09.

126

LETTER NUMBER 46

Three Pages to Al by Ivan at Darkside Goulburn C.C. 13th August 2009

G'day Alistair,

Hey, you were spot-on what the police use Google Earth for—your letter of 1 August spoke of how the police must use that Google Earth to come at them. You spoke of the raids on bike clubs that went down in Melbourne. I seen it on the TV news, as you say they took cars and Harleys as well. They found guns, drugs, as they always do when raiding bikies. Of course I know fuck all about Google Earth except what I see on TV, papers, but you say what we see is a couple of months' old shit. But probably the police get the pictures a bit earlier, and you mention that they (police) mustn't be able to turn it around.

To check back or they would have got the ones blowing up ATMs. Well today, the 13th, I see on the news the police have raided a dozen places and grabbed a heap of people for those ATM jobs. It seems you are right and they may be using it like a CCTV and can backtrack it and see where those people were from. I'm sure they will never reveal what they did to catch those cunts, but as I read your

127

letter and watch the news about them busting the ATM bandits, I think you are onto it.

And that bootlegging shit as you call it, crims being able to pay tax for what they think they made while doing their business and then they're left alone to keep going—I hear about people paying to get a green light to go on. I've heard of it before; a couple of the boys here did it and they eventually busted them, just let them get big enough to fuck them right up and lock them away. Yes, that's how it goes—a couple of people in here who mentioned something as you describe, and the ones who don't pay get busted and others pay and give others up.

Sometimes big people—politicians—get caught. That prick a couple of weeks ago in Queensland took heaps in bribes and was given up. He got seven years prison; I imagine he will be trying to do a deal to get out a bit earlier by giving up others.

The gronks on those walk-and-talk-and-see tours of this place are selected pro-government types and probably work in government jobs and get told all sorts of shit, why this place is run as it is, like you see what they say about me and how I am the worst cunt about. They see the commissioner of prisons saying that shit on the news about me; the gronks then hear it again as they walk around here. They can only think that we in here are really bad pricks.

I see they, police/DPP, are now charging all the bikies involved in that brawl at Sydney Airport with murder. I doubt if it will really stick when it goes to trial, as they have to show intent to murder. It can be reduced if they say they got involved in a fight okay but had no intent to actually kill anyone, but then they get hit with intent to cause grievous bodily harm, and that brings a big wack.

128

One cannot underestimate the fuck-up tricks that they use. And as you say, most people just sit back and don't believe all the shit that goes on, like I just watched those cops that morning in when they arrested me. They did whatever they wanted to and when it started to come undone at the trial, the prosecutor went on about something else and the fucked judge (who was a first-class dope) went along with it.

That's why now because these government pricks use the media to put shit on me and rubbish the fuck out of me,

And then all that bad publicity is used against me in here by management—they point it out to me and say it's the public.

Now I simply don't give a fuck. I've written twice now in the last 3 to 4 months to the minister of corrective services and said that they have to give me something meaningful to do in here after near-on eight years of just fucking sitting in a corner here. I've had it and it has to change.

Well Woodham replied to me about my first letter, a lot of fucken attitude. In effect he was telling me to just cop it. He said it's under his orders that I get fuck all, and Darkside HRMU is not like other places.

I sent his letter on to the High Court with a reminder letter by me about those matters that I raised that led me to chew off my finger. The court replied quite quickly that they are really considering my matter (yes, the cunts hate it, they don't like it at all as I am upsetting their rules—well, tough).

Whether my mind is fucked completely with putting up with all this isolation shit and being treated like a fucken dog, I don't know, and I know I don't care anymore and

129

I'm only waiting for a little while and I don't care what I have to do to myself.

What about the Chinese prick, chopped up his missus (another Asian person) and threw the bits off that big bridge on the freeway (pheasants' nest)? Crazy.

In regards to your mum and her health, parts failing, etc., of course they are, but certain parts are critical and some are not and will last forever as no load on them and they adjust to one's needs. You appear to realise this. My parts are also old but are still working okay (I hope). It's not like it is getting some new part that will be overwhelming to other parts; it's just another piece that hasn't got as many miles up as hers, so remind her of this.

I watch our government; they are good at making out that they care, like sending half our air force to New Guinea, to pick up nine dead Australians. One can feel sorry for the poor relatives, but no matter whether the government sends the fucken navy as well, those relatives are still going to cry. They do that shit and pay $200 million to Holden (under cover), and Holden then buys out that Ford V8 supercar (Vodaphone) team to switch to Holden. Hey, Al, you certainly live in a weird world out there.

So thanks again, Al, you are going okay, on top of most things, aware of what they can do (that's mad, the Google Earth shit). My regards to all of your family (it's bloody cold up here as well), and so you may you all stay warm and flu free, and wellness and good spirit be with you all.

Best regards and respect, Ivan. 13/August/2009.

LETTER NUMBER 47

One Page to Al from Ivan at Darkside Goulburn C.C. 2nd September 2009

Greetings Al,

And may all be fine with you and family. Okay, yes, I see that on the news, the cops raiding places that they allege have links to bikie clubs, to disrupt cash flow! Fuck—what cash flow these days?

That Google is hot stuff—the cops use it in a number of ways. They only have to show, say, a vehicle near one of those ATM areas, and then show the same type of vehicle at one's home—very circumstantial and very difficult to defend an allegation. Of course talk on phones, cars about jobs—well, that's not so clever.

Well that's a given that the cops will hassle-load that bloke up with shit charges to get him talking about that reb shoot-up in the workshop.

I see the cops have made a re-enactment of that bikie brawl—Sydney airport. It appears one of those involved in that shit has turned mutt and so a pantomime was videoed

131

of what he is now saying, as you say, it was rather stupid to do that at that airport.

For sure that bomber Lockerbie! Blew that jumbo out of the sky is laughing now, well the poms want some of that Libyan oil. So they let him go; it's the government way.

At the moment things are not real good with me. They all fucking me about, the courts still very reluctant to assist me and no word as to my reasonable requests by them, and of course the government will make sure I get fuck all and the prison bosses treat me like an arsehole, so I'm fucked every way, so now I don't give a fuck.

I've tried to be reasonable and go along with the system, but in my case they just keep on fucking me, so my mind has said fuck it all. I say nothing to them and just sit here. It's been a while since I have had something to eat, and for sure that is really fucking me now. I panic at times but, really, why should I just put up with this shit, just to make them look good? I don't know when, but my mind keeps me on this fucked course.

So thanks again, Al. You're going okay, and may it continue and also for your family. My regards and best respects to you, Ivan 2/9/09.

LETTER NUMBER 48

Two Pages to Al by Ivan at Darkside HRMCC Goulburn.

Goulburn NSW 2850 11th October 2009

G'day Alistair,

Oh yes, that recent South Australia court decision that it was unconstitutional to have control orders on bikies clubs will cause a rethink on how to legislate such laws. Parliaments (federal or state) are empowered to make the laws and are totally accepted as the law, but are subject to a challenge as a right in court, especially if they are unfairly biased or infringe on some basic rights. I believe that those South Australian bikie control orders were deemed unfair in that the police commissioner himself could decide which club or person would be hit with a control order.

I seen that red dust thing on the news—yes, it did look rather hectic. No real effect on us in here, Darkside

133

HRMCC, but must have really spread a lot of that red shit over everything in the town. I see on the local news that the council relaxed its water hose laws for a few days so all the shit could be washed away.

For sure that leb family, the Ibrahams, who supposably are really clever in what they do, yet now a lot are in prison and the millions hidden in the ceiling because they blabbed everything on their phones.

There are a few in here, and they rely on talking Leb when they discuss things.

I'm sure this place has bugs galore in where they congregate together.

That's fucked, bad news about the Warthog now moving in on Bodge, as the Warthog has a habit of conning people to go guarantee on loans that he gets. He did this to Mum once—got her to act as the guarantee on his loan and then fucked off and left Mum in the shit.

I suppose he lost his own place because he couldn't afford it; he was paid a bit of money by the media to put shit on me, but that couldn't have been enough to pay everything, and perhaps he thought that the media would keep on talking to him, as he was the only one in the family who spoke against me. The media knew he was all bullshit and nothing new can be said, so now he has lost everything and moved in on Bodge.

I'm really fucken myself in here right now. I simply cannot accept the bullshit that goes on in here. They run it as a punishment centre—we cannot get the normal stuff that other maximum security prisons get. After eight years I give up. I've complained to prison management, the minister, the prison commissioner, the ombudsman about it, they don't give a fuck so fuck it.

I rely on 3 to 4 slices of dry bread most days or some crushed up Weetabix (no milk) or slice up an apple. I dump the main meals, lunches and evening meals—this has been going on for a month now and I really have trimmed myself down a lot. I feel fucked.

Difficult to sleep, always fucken hungry, the guards here don't notice. I don't really talk to them and keep my head down; at times it's quite scary, as I know this diet, no veggies, meat, no real nourishment, is not doing me any good, but I cannot help myself. Some mornings I am surprised that I am still alive.

So, Al, thanks again for the mail. Despite the shit I do to myself in here, I still battle on to get justice, so my regards to all (tell them to keep an eye on that Warthog—he will rip Bodge off).

You stay well, and best regards and respect to you, Ivan 11 October 2009.

LETTER NUMBER 49

Three Pages to Al by Ivan at Darkside Goulburn C.C. 23rd November 2009

Hello, my friend Alistair,

And thanks for the mail of 10 November. Well yes, that mild protest that I was on, to eat only the barest, minimum food, was a slow version of suicide. And was really knocking me about but got used to it. It went on for over two months—all this was to highlight a wish that I be given some reasonable tasks to do in here, to keep one's mind occupied a bit; for over eight years it's been a case of simply sitting in here and rotting away.

So I asked and even wrote out requests for something to do; I tried management in here—, they are unable to make a decision, as they act only on orders from W woodham and co, from Sydney and, of course,

Macquarie Street – Parliament House. The politicians like to keep this place like a gulag so I write to them, no good, so I went on that self-starve diet, which was slowly wrecking me. And last week I was given seemly a reasonable bit of shit to occupy myself. Put me in the library one arvo to put stickers, etc., on the books, I knew,

136

as they put me there, it was bullshit more as one is lucky if one gets in there once a fortnight and sure enough I haven't been back there since, and no mentions of it.

That evening, I did in response to that offer take all my meals and have continued to do so since as I see that they simply lie and treat me like an arsehole, so I will build up my strength and show them that, well, I will act like an arsehole. Mild weak protests don't work, so a much more meaningful message is necessary.

I need my willpower with me on this, but I know what I will do, and one morning I will say today is the day. Currently I'm really fucked, very weak, even my feet causing pain—one's really swollen. No idea what but hopefully can regain some condition to ready myself for next protest at this place.

Well if they did place bugs, and I suspected they did, as they do it on lots of acres way before my arrest, but in my case it did not do them any good—all their 24-hour surveillance, visual phone taps, eaves listening devices, etc. Revealed that I lived a normal life, there was not one word or film-tape recording that was used against me.

Yes, those blokes in WA, 3 brothers—gold bullion robbery—fraud! The police framed them, but they never gave up (Mickleberg brothers), and it took them 25- to 30-plus years to overcome it. I admire those people who never give up. I'm not giving up.

I know what the government arseholes do and have no intention of ever stopping, and along the way I take on corrective services as these pricks work in with the government to give me a different time. Well one finger at a time—I suppose I don't give a fuck at what I do, as if it's necessary than it is not an unwise choice.

137

Yes, Detective Leach, he was a first-class prick all right and undoubtedly really was frightened of someone talking, as it was he (Leach) who was the face, who actually orchestrated the planting of evidence against me. If he ever spoke up, a lot of coppers would go down, Clive Small amongst them.

I am aware of some of that talk of that copper who shot himself (Bowral) and supposedly in remorse over his crimes and others (his old man—also a copper) covered it up. They cremated the body so they couldn't do a DNA on him; they could have got his toothbrush and did his DNA with that, but no. Because his father was a head copper, they covered it all up.

I hear his father went and seen his girlfriend, Debbie Francis, who said she had the jacket and watch that belonged to the German backpackers. She said he gave them to her, and told her he wanted all his clothes she had and she never knew him, so he destroys all evidence that could have been used. As you know he was suspected of the Bulli rapist and the Belanglo murders.

She rang Crime Stoppers and tried to make a scene about the jacket and watch; she was shut down. She eventually got someone to listen to her but it was all shut down real quick.

Most people are scared to pursue the matter. Well I'm trying to get an inquiry going. The Supreme Court being the review court, they use their exalted position to tell lies and dismiss my arguments as worthless.

Well it took me to chop my finger off to get the High Court even to respond to my correspondence, and they are very reluctant to give me reasonable go. I'm still chasing it

138

up; they go real slow, whether it's on purpose or just how it is, I still do write up query letters to them asking how it is proceeding.

Bad publicity, well, it certainly follows me. Last week or so I see on the news, 30 years ago in 1979, two young girls (15 or 16 years old) went missing, said they're meeting friends. This is in Wollongong, never returned.

Parents report it, police said probably runaways, and a couple of days later parents get letters from the girls. They're hand-written saying that they were with friends, the police seemingly accepted this and so did every other person, parents, but now 30 years later the government has a miserable $100.000 reward for information. Channel Nine, their news story showed film of me and that I was a suspect and said police investigated me but cannot find a link. Well I know where I was in 1979—no coppers ever spoke to me of this. I was never aware of this matter till last week.

That even happens in here. I wipe a lot of pricks off my list because they act like arseholes on some issues; it's fair enough against the guards but on one of us, it's not on.

Thanks again. My regards and respect to you, Ivan. 23/11/2009.

LETTER NUMBER 50

A Bit of Read over Xmas to Al from Ivan at HRMC Darkside Goulburn 15th December 2009

G'day Alistair, my friend,

Well in here I had a swollen foot, really ballooned up and hurt to put weight on it,
Yet nothing broken. Anyway in the end the doc had a look at it; the swelling went down and disappeared, but he sent me out to the outside hospital, Goulburn, to get one of those scan things, like what they use on mums-to-be to show trace the little bub in there. Well it can be used for all sorts of things to see what is inside one.

No one said nothing to me what was there, but next day I'm taken for X-rays, X-ray stomach, still no one tells me what are there looking for. And about a few days ago, 11th Dec., the squad (they took me to the Goulburn hospital also) came in and gave me a very fast ride to Sydney, Prince of Wales Hospital.

When they take me on these outside prison trips, they put me in those orange fluoro overalls, chains, and shackles as you can imagine; at this Prince of Wales hospital, I am in a wheelchair and six guards wheel me about the place. We got some looks, I tell you.

And I was placed on this machine; it sorta slides inside itself and an outside beam revolves around and scans you. In this case they only scan my stomach. The whole process only took five minutes, but there and back took five hours of a fast driving 3-vehicle convoy, and travel a lot faster than everyone else. Still no word as to what the fuck's wrong with me, like it has to cost thousands and thousands every day to take me out of this prison, and no cunt's telling me anything at all.

The Prince Of Wales Hospital is a real big place, lots of corridors, rooms, wards, etc., even made it up to the ninth floor for a while, ocean views. But alarming that everyone I can see in the place, the patients! Everyone seems old (I'm old as well), so it must be one of the last places people get to see? Pick up their one-way ticket to bye-bye!

The High Court finally agreed that I send in my appeal application as is. Handwritten documents and send it by the mail, this is the reason I chop my finger off—to show how difficult it is for a prisoner in HRMCC to meet High Court rules.

So I get the prison management to photocopy everything I am sending to the High Court; they said I need five sets of everything, so photocopying cost me $618 (I expected $1200 to $1300, but prison management said they used both sides of each page). Fuck, I hope the court says it as their rule is print one-side only.

141

So I sent it by registered mail. Quite a bundle to High Court, they want three complete sets; it weighed 4.75 KG and cost $13.00 for postage. So finally I have this appeal moving along at last.

Anyway, Al, it was great to hear from you, I'm still battling on and expect to take the battle forward, especially about their fucken place, but will make sure my appeal is on track, plus I'm still getting over that starvation protest I did. That fucked me up a bit but am slowly getting some condition back.

So X-mas is on—you enjoy it with your family. Hope your mum is fine and of course old Santa is kind to you as well.

Take care on the road (I couldn't believe how many cars are on the road now). And so thanks for the support. Best regards and respect, Ivan. 15/Dec/2009.

LETTER NUMBER 51

Two Pages to Al by Ivan at Darkside Goulburn C.C. 24th January 2010

Hello Al,

Good to receive your letter of 9th January. I always appreciate the news in it, and may all be fine with you and your family.

Things are still very ordinary in here and, oh yes, you deserve that my mail, all mail out or in, is thoroughly looked. Well it keeps them awake, I suppose, and in a job.

Woodham and co wants to privatise most of the prison system; he reckons too much money wasted on shit things. Eventually he might get his way, but I don't care either way; I can live with him being pissed off a bit.

I laughed at that bit with the Warthog; if he carks it, get Bodge to ring your mum immediately. I'm sure he will do that and I'm sure you can get a firsthand look at whatever goodies there is to be got at.

And no doubt at all the Warthog went to the enemy over your mum.

Late in '07, two of them arseholes came in here to see me. I was taken to the interview room in cuffs, they introduced themselves. One of the pricks even put his hand out to shake my hand.

So they said that they look at old cases and had been talking to the Warthog (they referred to his name as Boris) and that he had gave them a lot of information about me. One of the pricks was setting up a tape recorder and had six tapes lined up—good grief, he must have had high hopes. The other one had these folder/book-lots of typed-up statements? And read them out, including a shooting of some garage!

Person in mid-sixties and all sorts of other crimes. I just sat there and did not say one word, no acknowledgement of anything. This pissed them off—one prick started to get shitty then both after thirty minutes they fucked off, and I've never heard anything more about any of the shit that they were on about.

That High Court appeal application—it is a question of law only. They are not deciding on guilt or innocence but whether that review (Supreme Court) judge can rule how he did. The law is that he is wrong, but you know what they do at times. If it ruled wrong, then it goes back to the Supreme Court and they look again at my application for an inquiry into my conviction, so I can just wait and see what the High Court decides. They could look at it anytime, even take a year or more.

Yes I didn't mind that Sydney trip, even trussed up the way I was lots of traffic (lots of small cars about, and as you say lots of Indians-Arabic-China types driving and

144

basically owns the footpaths in areas as I travel through. Like if I was asleep and then woke and seen the shops and people, I could have thought we were in Jakarta or Delhi. Even the hospital I went to, 9 out of 10 hospitals personnel (doctors, nurses, cleaners, etc.) that I seen were from god knows.

In here, Darkside, the majority are from some other country, lots of Muslims; it's not a concern at all for me, as I'm confined in segregation. Solitary. Of course they buy up a lot of homes, they love the place. Those government home grants, extra incentives, they put in double families and charge big rents, no problems for them. I don't think it makes any difference what government is in power, the boaties will risk it and are willing to spend 2 to 3 years in detention centres, and then most are given residence in Australia. They have nothing to lose; they leave there own shitty country because their government shoots, hangs and executes them on anytime. No wonder Australia is such a good place for them.

So my friend, thanks again. You going okay and stay cool. Teach Jess the tricks of life, say hello to your mum and family and all to stay safe. Hectic out there at times.

My best regards and respect, Ivan 4/January/2010.

LETTER NUMBER 52

Two Pages to Al from Ivan at Darkside Goulburn C.C. 24/2/2010

G'day Al,

Good to receive your 15th Feb. letter on the 22nd. And yes and yes, I did hear/see on the news that some rain has fallen upon some areas near Sydney. For sure your garden would have loved it.

An unwelcome surprise for those South Australian blokes through only a momentary event it sorted them out and that explosion as you say it will have an effect on the authorities to shut down the all bikies gangs. Though it will stop a lot because they (the police) will target individuals and some, as you realise, will not want the unnecessary attention. Business will still carry on for those in the so-called business, though without hiding in bikie gangs.

What about that shitty TV show a couple of weeks ago, very anti-bike and featured our "Rebel" friend, though in here it would only have increased his status? And that supposably masked "notorious" gang member, spilling his guts, his reference to the gang handbook as to how to

146

conduct one's illegal business, recipes to make drugs to sell on the street, etc.? The TV people certainly make up a story to discredit bikie gangs.

That's good news, so no issue with the taxman to delve into, for sure it was that anti-bikie taskforce people that would have sic(ed) the tax man on to you; undoubtedly some will get caught out, and that leaves it open for an attempt to confiscate things of being proceeds of crime

The Warthog and interviews (to police and media)—I now am seeing Channel 9 promoting some new shitty program, *Crime Families*? Something like that, supposedly on when the Olympics finished. They feature me and speak of how the family are into crime? They are to raise the criminal history of the family? I am not sure how viewable that will be as except for a stolen car or break and enter and all this about forty years ago? Of course a story could be made of Bodge's 1973 Quanta's job, where he tried to extort them for $200.000, but seeing as he was 14 years old, I cannot imagine it, but as you know the media arseholes put a lot of shit on the situation and make out that it's fact. I can't believe the law fell for it—he was a kid playing a joke.

Bill told me a couple of months ago that some TV mob was offering cash to the family for interviews, so naturally the Warthog will jump at that and of course George said $350 he got, so George works pretty cheap. Oh yes, I imagine a lot of shit put on me is bad enough, but I get pissed off when I see them belittling the family.

As usual things are still fucked in here—Darkside is totally separate from the main prison. Double walls, razor barriers, gates, the usual shit, and was put in orange overalls, leg shackles, security belt and handcuffed to this

147

belt, like I am only going to the clinic-hospital in main prison, yet I'm escorted by four guards. One even held onto the belt, like all this shit for a five-minute walk to the doctor, like all of Goulburn prison is maximum-security prison. Darkside is set in a corner of it, yet they carry on with this shit. I had nothing better to do and at least got five minutes of sun and could only think that whoever thinks of this shit would have to be an "absolute moron." Like we are in a high-security prison yet on a hundred-yard walk it took four people plus chains, cuffs, orange overalls just for that.

It keeps one amused at such things. (Fucken stupid, really) At least the doc told me that. Those pre-X-mas trips outside hospitals Goulburn and Sydney for X-mas scans, etc., revealed nothing, and I have to go again for more tests in Sydney. Well I don't feel I will be doing that.

I also do fuck all, just sit in here day in, etc., day out, etc.! No wonder I continually spend hours each day and night working out ways to injure myself.

That occupies me for a while, and it's a really weird system that I basically have to fuck up parts of myself to get something to occupy myself.

And back about the Warthog, a lot of people are aware of what he is and no matter what they may say, though it may sound good and very damning to me, he is fucked to give any specific details; he is like those media journalists who write up a lot of bad shit about me but can never refer to proof or whatever.

So, Alistair, my thanks again. My regards to your mum and family, and you keep yourself fine. Best regards and respect.24/2/2010.

148

LETTER NUMBER 53

Two Pages to Al by Ivan at Darkside Goulburn C.C. 23rd March 2010

Hey Alistair and hello,

As you say the club scene as it was for the last decade or more is gone and any that stays, as it was conduct themselves like the old days as you and others had. Well they are easy targets for the police; they have the politicians making shit laws to suit the police and government cheer squad (the fucken media) prints, talks the government shit about bikies, the clubs, so unless someone gets elected into Parliament that is a dead-set bikie no more, as you know it.

That's how the Warthog works—tell lies to suit himself, and fuck everyone else. It shows what an absolute moron he is at his age, no prospects, no home of his own, no place to call home, no solid family life, absolutely none, no friends. The only place he would have a friend is in prison because he would be in the boneyard (protection) with a lot of other dogs just like him.

I don't feel sorry at his position; he has nothing, gets a bit of attention only because he is a dog and does what the media tells him to do. Of course they pay him for it, but he soon runs out of dough and has to move on.

You got your place. Friends, family, and Dick spoke to that television mob; they were paid for it. It's called *Families of Criminals*, or something like it. Perhaps Dick may think that he will be able to tell his own story—that is what he may have been told and agreed to it. I suppose the cash money was a big incentive as well, but those TV mongrels would sell their own mothers to make up a story. I think it will be made to look like Dick is guilty. They will use what he says, cut out a bit, turn it around so he looks bad, and that's the aim of this TV program. To appreciate family as being involved in what I got convicted for.

It won't affect me; no matter what shit they say, it already been said and all it does is get me more fan mail. A lot of crazy pricks out there like that shit.

Our friend, his story on *Gangs of Oz*, the bikie shooting that gained him a lot more attention, as some people had no idea of what he did (shooting four bandidos), and that TV show made show made him look bad in the eyes of a lot who believe all they see on TV. You know all this and why it is done.

I feel about fucked with it all and cannot accept their persecution anymore and don't give a fuck about my health and well-being anymore. I take all my meals and dump 95 percent of it, been doing it for about a week and a half now. Lost a bit of condition, of course. I live on milk, ice blocks, mainly, and seem to keep me going okay. I do nothing except sit in here all day so don't need much energy and appear to be fine and it permits my mind to accept the shit that they do to me in here.

150

So besides feeling a bit crook and I cannot complain about that, as I don't know if it is what I'm doing to myself or have real health issues, either way at the moment I don't really care.

Yes, it was quite an eye-opener those days out and out in the main would be, in last twelve-odd years, the only crowd that I have been in is when the screws come into cell area, five-six or more.

So, Al, thanks for the mail (your letter of 8th of March, received the 19th). Give my regards and respect to your mum and others. You stay cool and well.

Best regards and respect, Ivan 23/3/2010.

LETTER NUMBER 54

All Three pages by Ivan at Darkside Goulburn HRMCC 27th April 2010

G'day Alistair,

Williams getting whacked, of course, yes, a paid hit and not with standing at has been said as how it occurred (CCTV footage, etc.). That person who allegedly committed the hit can raise a fairly credible defence once (if it does) get to the courts, then self-defence (fear, etc., of CW) and no intent? Actually had called the sleepy guards to save him? It can be another good story.

Intel people! Failed to return your call regarding visit application. Well he's probably very busy reading other people's mail? A squad of them does that, and that's why the mail when it gets to you (or others) looks very second-hand (well read).

And, Al, that's what the Warthog does to anyone that fronts him about his dodgy ways (rip off Bodge, etc.). As your mum did well, that causes him to get back at them, and seemingly the Warthog used you to ring the police!

And once he mentioned the Rebels, motorcycle club, and possible drugs and weapons, etc., the police act and jump on you?

That is what he does—he's a real mutt. Early last year the detectives came in here to talk to me (not about murders, disappearances, etc.). But they had a book/folder an inch thick at least in which they said was statements from the Warthog (they did identify him to me) about old serious crimes from the sixties to early seventies, which I had allegedly committed. It included shootings, someone in a garage, break and enters, vehicles, attacks.

I did not make one comment about any of the shit. I did not acknowledge it and the presence of the police being put in the room with them, they both put their hand out, shake hands, and I ignored them and stayed silent for the whole meeting.

The fucking Warthog, and this is what he does.

Families of Crime! Yes, I did view it the other evening—what a shitty program. Of course the Warthog featured quite prominent in it (and I guess that you seen all this shit yourself).

Of course the program put shit on the whole family; the arseholes do that, the Warthog assists them by putting shit on Dad and Mum as well the old man did have some weird ideas but didn't carry on like the Warthog was making out.

Yes that really pisses him off about Cookie (Lysine). I'm the father of her and what fucks him over it, he had no idea, till Rare told Cookie in 1994 after my arrest, Cookie came and seen me about (I always got on good with her, this is in the late eighties to early nineties). Rare pissed the Warthog off, divorced him and rang me up.

153

I often went to Rare's place (Cookie lived there as well). Cookie got thirty thousand dollars off *New Idea* magazine for her story. Five pages of nothing really were amazing!

So the Warthog had no idea. He said a lot of shit, he always does and plainly he was following a script made up by that TV people.

And what about George, also no respect. Like he looked like an arsehole and surely showed it (probably even got ripped off by that TV mob, they were paying everyone money to appear). Very disappointing George was, but when you are an arsehole you are an arsehole, and he sure showed the world what he is.

Bodge looked okay, I thought ageing very well and spoke well, though probably had no idea of what he was being asked.

Loved Dick (Richard)—he got into their faces, quite excellent, always is despite the media putting shit on him. I thought Dick did well.

The whole show smacked of desperation by its makers to show me, the family in some bullshit way. Hillbillies—what shit they put up.

Clive Small looked very ordinary and as usual relied upon lies to make his story and of course the usual the other arseholes who get paid to say whatever.

A rather poor quality program, I thought, and I suppose it would have appealed to some who believe what they see on TV media. I'm sure it will be re-run often and so family and I are always in the news.

Lots of informers out there as well as in here, all walks of life. I see that some cunts gave up a senior screw (that prison out near Windsor!).He was bringing in stuff at very high prices and was given up and they have him at ICAC, and he in turn is spilling his guts.

(I got a letter recently from the premier department.) They refer to their policy, I had been complaining of it in here. It seems I have to do a bit more, and because I am about fucked, health-wise and in here, their policy is that I just sit and rot slowly away in here. Well, fuck, I find it difficult to accept and I must be a bit insane (every tenth one! Warthog!), so I guess insanity will permit me to cope with the shit and I really got nothing to lose.

So ratbag TV programs may get some cunts excited—it only increases my hatred because management uses that shit on TV to make sure that they are seen to be real arseholes when it comes to me, so I get fuck all, all the time.

I can be a real arsehole hillbilly very easy and I am being consumed by that thought.

Your letter 20th April, photos, were received the 25th, and thanks a lot, Al. I always seal my letters, but the readers (Intel) seemly don't and probably even told me that my mail generally does look very second-hand by the time they get it.
Give my regards to all. Keep alert, best regards with respect, 24/4/2010.

155

LETTER NUMBER 55

Two Pages to Al by Ivan from my Sunless Cement Cave.

Darkside Goulburn C.C.18th May 2010

Hello Alistair,

Giddy and glad to know that all appears fine with you and your family.

I see on the news tonight the NSW government have changed the law on proceeds of crime; they (police) can ask now where did the cash come from!

I've been told George got $2,500-plus, and they gave him a carton of beer and probably got him half pissed and told him what to say. I thought it was a weird interview. Only his face was shown (probably had a beer in his hand!). (George is cheaply brought—I was told the Warthog got more than double.) That's twice he's told bad lies for cash and because he is a dope he is not aware of the dishonour he's showing to the family.

I'm here in my cement cave, no cunt gives a shit in here, but for the family out there that what George says reflects on all of them all.

And as you know, most are pissed off at him, like all is aware of what an arsehole the Warthog is, as it's not only me he puts shit on, but he's turned on quite a few of you out there. I've never given a shit about the Warthog and what he says as he can say a lot but it's all bullshit and it may sound bad when he speaks about me. You and others out there have to be wary of him. The police would love him, as he is so willing to put people in. (In my case, he had dozen of pages about me, but it's plain the police worked with the Warthog. They told him of all these offences that they never solved and expected me to confess to them?) As he showed on TV film, he is very hostile to all of you as well as me.

As you say Dick is fairly well laid back, I reckon that fucken Crown Prosecutor Tedeschi from my trial would love to get Dick up on a charge. He had Dick there on the stand for days and Dick was on him, in his face.

It's getting worse in here even though we do fuck all, but like that shit that went down with that underbelly bloke # Carl Williams get whacked to death in that Victorian prison, well the next day in here they banned any association with others out in places where two could get together for an hour or so.

I'm battling to stay sane in here and I'm losing that battle as well; it takes its toll on me every day.

157

I sent in another application for an inquiry into my conviction the other day (registered mail) to the Supreme Court, conviction the other day (registered mail) to the Supreme Court. I'm allowed to do this; it will be number four and they, the attorney general, Crown department, courts, will hate it as they again have to come up with bullshit to get over it.

I used what was said by the review judge in my last one in 2008, I was arguing that they the Crown used non-existent evidence to make their case out against me. That explained away the DNA evidence; it never implicated me, and the fucken prosecutor tried to say it was contaminated or belonged to someone else, so they come up with there was another person or persons doing the murders with me. But that was never proved and the jury did not have to decide my guilt on it.

But I have been on to the courts for an inquiry into this or others was involved with me, so the judge ends up saying "it was never to the Crown's case that others may have been involved."

Well I am entitled to request an inquiry as long as I have new evidence that I can point to. So I realised that that Supreme Court judge raised new evidence for me, at my trial I was fucked as I was relying on the DNA—it wasn't mine so I never did it. But once they said that there must have been someone else with me, I was fucked and no matter what I said I couldn't get over this other or others with me. So I made up a pretty good argument in No. 4 petition, as so it will piss them off a bit.

Anyway, Al, thanks again for the mail. You keep on top of things, be wary of the Warthog, etc.

Good luck with things and best regards and respect, 18/May/2010.

Then can pass new laws to force people where the money comes from, but here I am asking where is that evidence you (the Crown) said of another person or persons—did it exist? Or was it a lie? I have Supreme Court judges lying about it now.

LETTER NUMBER 56

Two Pages to Al by Ivan from Cement Cave in Darkside Goulburn C.C. 28th June 2010

Hello Alistair,

G'day, thank you for the 18th June mail received the 27th, and may all be fine with you and your family.

Quite cold already—no matter how rugged up one is, there is a risk of catching a cold.

It's cold here; our cement caves would make an Eskimo shiver. Prison overcrowding, etc., I see that shit on the news, whether it's correct, I don't know? There are a lot of folks in prison. I think the government arseholes are more concerned at the cost of it.

Not of how many there is, well over a billion dollars a year for 10,000 prisoners, and if more comes in, another prison is needed and so another 200-odd million to build it, plus the dough to run it.

They fucked things up with their grand ideas, big sentences—more prisons and this place, triple the normal

160

cost, not that I care about it, not many in here but lots of screws to run it, so now they will keep a lot more out there, detention centres—yeah, as if that will cause any problems for anyone (go to the boozer then stop at the hospital and say you have a headache or some shit, Attorney General Hatzistergos is a real shithead and will fuck it up, as everything he does is fucked). Look at bike gang laws!

I see at the moment that the matter is the High Court; I would think that it was well argued by the bikies' legal, and the court is considering the issue. I see the papers over this weekend ran some stories about it.

It does seem to be the go for the islanders to run amuck, especially out your way; nothing really clever about them, gangs up on someone and bashes the shit out of him, rob him and there laughing. Perhaps one day someone will get sick of it and pull out a gun and whack a couple—that may deter them!

I see some old bloke up New Castle way pulled his gun out and gunned to death, a couple of his neighbours who it seems had fronted him over some shit. He fucked up by giving himself up and for his stand he will get life, but he did what he had to.

Not much going on in here as usual, I complain to relevant minister but really have to do a lot more to get turfed out of here. At the moment am waiting what the Crown solicitors will say in reply to my latest Supreme Court petition for judicial inquiry into my convictions. I finally got word from the court that they sent on my submissions/petition, etc., to the attorney general's department.

The prison fucked around with my mail for a while before it was sent to court; that pissed me off and had

161

feared I had to damage to my health and body in protest over it. It's all I can do when they pull that shit on me.

I'm sure the Crown solicitors will not like my argument that I raise for an inquiry, they will reject it, but it will angry them as I use their legal bullshit reasons.

This shit is about all that I do in here, and about the only reason I don't chop out a few more body parts (I don't think in their mad-section hospital they allow writing materials?).

Hopefully you have sorted out your computer problems by now. I had put down on my last activity buy-up sheet (we can buy runners, some clothing, and other shit every month or so) I put down for a laptop. I seen this brochure in one of the papers and so chose the top unit ($2599.00 cost)—seems to have everything in it (even an old, shitty typewriter would do me). I put it in, later I was told it's not on! How disappointing that was!

Anyway, Al, thanks again. Good to know that you ok.
Hopefully still are and family.
My regards to your mum. Stay well and best regards with respect, Ivan. 28/6/2010.

LETTER NUMBER 57

Two Pages to Al from Ivan in my Cement Cave, Sunless and Cold, Darkside Goulburn C.C. 26th July 2010

Hello Alistair,

Good to hear from you, and your writing program seems to be operating very well. Thank you for the mail of 16 July 24th.

Of course the Warthog still being an arsehole, always was and causing hassles for others to get his way, rubbishing your mum, that's his style. I cannot believe anyone in the family (except shithead George) would believe what he says. I think it is the Warthog's plan to keep your mum away from Bodge? It wouldn't surprise me if he were planning some dodgy plan to make out that he owns the place and or possibly con Bodge into signing up for something for the Warthog.

Perhaps Mary or whoever forgets how the Warthog conned Mum to guarantee for some of his dodgy business plans. So he puts shit on your mum, and no one else is there to keep an eye on things. You have to be wary of him, as he has that propensity to talk to the police and put any lie out about things. I'm not concerned about the prick myself, but he can cause problems for Bodge.

I had a bit of a win yesterday, Sunday the 25th. The Sunday *Sun* ran an article about me and my battles for justice; they referred to a letter that I wrote about it. The frame-up. The courts on appeals covering up the miscarriage of justice. I was quite pleased at it; Bill sent it in for me—on page two of the paper as well.

They did not print what I wrote about Clive Small framing me or the parts that Bill also wrote, but it was quite a change to see me in the paper and not be accused of another murder, a shitty picture but and wouldn't you know it, Al, the reporters for some reason, at the end of my article, spoke to the prison commissioner Woodham, well, what a corrupt arsehole he is, a real vindictive mutt. He uses his position to deny me proper procedures; he said I will never leave Darkside: "He is going to stay there."

Like what a limited vocabulary the prick has, I was raising issues about miscarriage of justice—courts covering up dodgy evidence, and not mentioning the place and how it is run, yet Woodham simply acts like a real dope and raves on how will never get out of here.

I read your summary on how screws are, and, yes, Woodham is exactly like that. And he will find out that I will disappoint him and that I can be a rat-bag like he is. I have nothing to lose that I care about and will do whatever I feel is necessary to prove Woodham is a rat-bag with no integrity and that he forces me into self-harm because he

164

uses his position wrongly against me. Your view of them is spot-on, and soon enough and soon enough I will do what I should not have to do, but it's the only way for me in here.

I still see the police is on to the bikie clubs and there is some attention being given by the media to court challenges. The courts tend to back legislation made by Parliaments and unless it can be shown to be against the public interest, it will stay as law.

As I see the bikers (legal-lawyers). Arguing that the anti-bikes laws can be used against anyone. (It probably can be construed to be like that!) But as I understand it, the law says it applies to bikie gangs and needs evidence to go before a judge to decide. So I cannot see the High Court doing much.

And on bikies, a friend of mine (out there) is reading that book *Blood Money*—it's about drugs, the drug wars and drug bosses, and she tells me there are some pages on the bikies and has a photograph of Alex Vella and says a bit about him and the Rebels.

I haven't seen this book yet but am aware that shithead Clive Small is involved with the book. They use his name on it, as can go on TV media, and he raves on about it. Your local library should have a copy (your mum might go to the library?). Don't go buying the book.

So, Al, thanks again. You're in good health to battle that—makes it easier to do it now! Keep Jess in line and do what you do to stay safe and on top, my best regards to your mum and all. Take care and best regards and respect, Ivan 26th JULY 2010.

LETTER NUMBER 58

Two Pages to Al by Ivan from the Sunless Cement Cave, Darkside HRMU Goulburn C.C. 10th August 2010

Hello Alistair,

Yes, they certainly lay it into me; anything I do in claiming innocence gets belittled, as I stated in my letter of 26th July about how the shitheads carried on. So thanks for the 25th July letter, received 5th of August—at least your print (computer) machine punches out your letters okay.

It is not a concern that those shitheads rubbish me because I claim innocence; at least my letter of innocence was printed in the biggest paper in Australia and probably elsewhere in Australia, even on that website I hear about. So people (some) may wonder a bit.

And other copies were sent on to other people—Bill did a good thing for me in that. You know how the media, they rubbish anyone that the government tells them to put

166

shit on, like they did hammer (you) bikies there for a while and will continue whilst the government/police tell them to do it.

What they have, Al, is *relevance deprivation syndrome* (RDS). In most cases, the fat prick got no attention so to look "relevant" they target someone who they know the media will react to in this case, me. So I write an innocence letter detailing a lot of facts involved in my conviction and court decisions and here is Woodham, to get some attention to be the centre of the media; he wants to be in the papers. Woodham says, "He will never get out of Darkside," fucken shithead who abuses his position and tortures me into self-harm.

I see one of the politicians get into that shit because she was pissed and refused to blow into the breath-analyse machine, like if they were clever (as they were 20 years ago) they would get out of it in a minute; as it is now even the dumbest copper is too frightened not to book a politician.

Well you're right about the white man not wanting to do the hard jobs now. I see that shit on TV, cut back and bring all the Indians, etc., into Australia. I notice the big mining company's whinge about it as they use them to work a lot cheaper.

I'm just sitting here in my sunless cave having a coffee and cake, the radios on some talk-back radio, and of course the commentators rubbish every poor bastard that the government rubbish, and then this bloke called Richard got on and raved on how labour will send everyone broke; he quoted some details. Sounded just like Dick, and I'm sure it was.

I'm still waiting to hear what the Crown solicitor (attorney-general department) has to say about my latest petition for an inquiry into my conviction.

The Supreme Court sent my petition to them and told me that they have till the end of August to submit a written reply to my submissions, and if I wish I can reply to that and when we all conclude our submissions, it will be given to a judge to act on. This is really the one thing that keeps me going in here, when I hear and read how Woodham uses his position to deny me normal access to the usual prison procedure. I in turn can be an arsehole as well and only am waiting for the court to send me the Crown's reply has me still in one piece.

Anyway, hopefully Joe can keep his business going in any way that he can. And that your mum is going okay, please send my best regards to her, and so also you keep travelling well and thanks again, Al. Best regards and respect, Ivan 10th August 2010.

LETTER NUMBER 59

Two Pages to Al by Ivan from my Sunless Cement Cave HRMU Darkside Goulburn C.C. 31st August 2010

The Warthog and his relevance deprivation syndrome wants the media to put him on TV, wants to be centre of attention, so he tells lies about me to get it.

Hello Alistair,

No presumption of innocence given to me, the media have pronounced me guilty of another murder. What a bunch of morons they are. So, Al, thank you for the mail your letter of 23rd of August, received the 29th, and may all be fine with you and your family.

Yes, the media pricks really laid it in to me and bullshit put to you folks out there. I see on the evening news one dopey bitch said that the police came in to question me about that skeleton hat was discovered in the Belanglo. Well they have not and never do. Not that I would be able to assist them—I have no knowledge of it and that's it.

Oh yes, way too long in here. It will be nine years on the 14th of September. Management regards me as an idiot, so I guess I have to act like one. I am not permitted to purchase anything to let me maintain my mental equilibrium which after nine years of just sitting in my sunless cement cave leaves me no choice.

Your power bill ($929)—I had often seen your letters telling me how pricey things are out there now but had no idea how really dear it is. The electricity bills are often mentioned on the news, how dear it is and going up all the time. That cost combined with rent, food, living expenses, etc. Yes, it would be difficult for a lot of folks and of course I get my three meals a day, no bills, no comfort, either. TV is all-digital now in all prisons; at least I have no bills—weekly buy-ups, they pay for it. And I cost about 1,300 to 1,400 dollars a day to keep confined in Darkside, very labour intensive (lots of screws per person—need 4 to 5 of them before they will open the cave doors).

Yes, quite a lot of lebs here, drugs, gangsters, or terrorists is what they are in for, not much company in here. Darkside is a segregation prison, at best—if it's permitted, one can associate with another one person for a couple of hours a day.

Bill did a good job getting my letter into the paper, my story of how the courts cover up my appeals. Cover up dodgy convictions. I have another petition (15/5/2010) with the Supreme Court to have a judicial inquiry into my case, the evidence used to convict me, did the Crown's primary evidence of another or other persons exists. The Crown in reply is supposed to send me their response to my submissions. I should get them by this weekend. It's all that keeps me intact in this place—waiting for that.

I watch some TV show last night 4 corners (ABC-1) had a story on drug gangsters—and of course bikers were

170

featured in it (comancheros) pretty flash mob! The dickhead Clive Small was in it, putting shit on everyone, practically the bike clubs.

Yeah, that Warthog, I fully expect that arsehole (or even shithead George) to go on the news to put shit on me about that skeleton in Belanglo. I guess the media hasn't been willing to pay his price. At least now there is this new Belanglo shit on the news now makes a bit of a change.

I hope your mum is going okay. This shit on TV (Belanglo) must be upsetting her. I hope not and so sorry that it is going on, but I know fuck all about it, and those media fucks just play the story up and because the police tell them nothing, they make up lies.

So, Al, I will do what I have to, piss them off a bit, but at my age I don't give a fuck, as there is little now that they can do to me. Keep Jess on track, you travel well, my regards to your mum, and I don't give a shit about what is being said on TV or about the Warthog. I thank you again. Best regards with respect, Ivan 3/8/2010.

LETTER NUMBER 60

One Page to Al by Ivan from my Sunless Cement Cave, HRMU Darkside Goulburn C.C. 2nd October 2010

Hello Al,

G'day, good to hear from you, and may it all still be fine with you and your family.

Yes, the Warthog tests one's patience, and he knows he is such a mutt, lets everybody in the family think he's a piece of shit. He even knows it, like fancy talking like that prick Clive Small does, but while the media pays him he will say whatever they want him to. So he will grab whatever he can and doesn't care what he has to do.

The usual shit going on in here. I sent off my reply to the Crown's submissions, I had put in an application for a review of my convictions (fourth one to date); the Crown made up twenty pages calling for the court to regret my application. I made up eight pages calling for the court to reject my application; I made up eight pages of rebuttal, lots of good argument. But very aware the courts will not expose their corrupt system and consider my matter fairly.

I heard that Woodham (prison commissioner) on the radio (Ray Hadley—talk-back) last Friday week and that prick Hadley asked him about me. Woodham said that I was in denial, won't accept my quilt.

Well Woodham's the one in denial, denies me reasonableness and I have had it and to cope with the shit I dump all my meals, been six days today and despite feeling a bit crook, I cope with everything to the screws about it. I live on coffee okay.

So thanks again, Al, you take it easy. I notice on the news that the police are still hassling the bikies, raids and other shit on some of them.

Give my regards to Mum. My best to you, Ivan 2/10/2010.

LETTER NUMBER 61

Two Pages to Al from Ivan from my Sunless Cement Cave.

HRMU Darkside Goulburn C.C. 5th December 2010

Sometimes it is more important to see, than what is said.

Hello Alistair,

Yes, that matter with Bill's nephew, a real heartache for all of us, affects a lot of families; it really shocked me and so sad for all involved.

I had heard about it on the news reports, and spite what is said in the papers, no screws, prison people or anyone spoke to me about it, and I certainly made no comments about it.

I only found out the following Saturday. Bill on a visit told me about who it was. I had no idea and as you may gather, I never got to meet the young bloke.

The media certainly carried on their usual arsehole way. I read all their shit, and of course the police will be glad as the media has young Mattie convicted. That ice shit sure has an effect? Bill said it and other stuff, which was being used.

So at least it has to be a lesson for some people. As now the other two is giving up young Mattie (it will be the police encouraging them, no one will be seeing sunlight for a long while if ever, any of them).

I see in Victoria (just had an election—new state government is now). And of course law/order was made an issue, lot worse there now than NSW, cut out a lot of non-prison options, I believe.

Oh yes, the new TV is a beaut. I suppose that's how they are now, access to all channels plus lots of stuff-information-things-no doubt you are familiar with it. (At least it costs me nothing.) And yes, I've been asking for a while for a laptop-type print machine. I don't want Internet access. We used to have computer print gear here but they removed it a year ago, very handy stuff as it kept one occupied, keeps mind busy, so I've asked for something instead of just sitting here. I cannot sit in here and carry on normally anymore.

I'll start sending Woodham some fingers first, so what I have been doing for a while is dumping all the main meals, no lunch or tea, no cooked/made-up meals. I survive on two slices of bread, a couple of handfuls of Weeties (dry) and bits of fruit or something. It keeps me in a real dopey state in that I don't care and can happily sit in here all day doing nothing; it knocks my health about, but I don't really worry about that.

I try to eat the least minimum that I think is necessary to keep me going. I was going real well on it, up to day 42 of my low-diet programs and had to come off it for a while,

175

to make up a new appeal to the Court of Criminal Appeal. It took me about three weeks to write it up, and I tell you my body really reacted to getting some decent amount of food. I didn't like it and it caused me considerable discomfort for the first fortnight, bloody terrible, but I completed the appeal all handwritten, based on "new evidence," "fresh evidence" and posted it off to the courts last week. Hopefully the prison sent it on, they hold up my registered mail to stuff me about—Woodham's orders, I suppose.

Anyway I am sure the court appeal won't like it and will cause me hassles and refuse to file it or shit like that, but I will deal with it no matter what they say.

So I'm now back on my low diet. I don't worry about the prison, as they don't really care what I do as long as I stay here is their only concern. I don't talk to them at what I do; they haven't got the authority and so why bother with them. In time I will write to Woodham again, but I want to get a lot more weight off yet.

No matter, Al, how happy you are, always keep all your property in your control—lots of people don't do that and lose a lot, so you know how it goes, stay in control.

Also my regards to your mum and family, and keep on top, Al. Regard and respect, Ivan 5th/December/2010.

LETTER NUMBER 62

Two Pages to Al by Ivan from my Sunless Cement Cave. HRMU Goulburn C.C. 31st December 2010

Hello Alistair,

G'day, and may this new year be good to you and family. Thank you for the mail of 14th Dec. (received the 26th) and for your kind thoughts and letters during the past year—very much appreciated, Al.

Yes, Bill's nephew (Mattie) certainly blew everyone away, and now we know it was a drug deal went wrong, which generally leads to one result (which it did). Of course the shitheads in the media carried on like absolute morons, and yes I did see a lot of their bullshit reporting, whether it's the papers, TV, radio or the Net, they are the same bubble-headed morons.

For sure the prison gets overcrowded (not in darkside—no crowds in here, except with screws), but I note that a lot get speared out on parole. They seem to sit a couple of times a week now (the list is in the papers—the low courts pages page), and one imagines at least 50 percent would get out.

I see in the news in California USD, 170,000 prisoners and the government spend more on prisons than on schools. Extraordinary, really, as at least there will be a couple of million kids at school, but that is how it is there and undoubtedly NSW will be aware of how much it costs and always going up in costs, so in soft cases such as yours there are lots of options for them (well, we can only hope it goes like that for you).

I am going quite well in my way that I cope with this place, dump all meals. Just eat a slice or two of bread or a handful of Weeties. Main food is I freeze the milk, ice blocks, but it's really causing heaps of problems, I think, but I seemly happy to keep doing it. Not one decent meal or hot meal or anything in December (today is day 33 of this). The guards seemly not aware of anything. I don't say anything, but what can I say, I am doing it myself and seemly it's working as I do nothing anyway, but now I simply don't care and the days just fly by. I'm half asleep most of the time, and don't give a shit now about anything in here.

Still no word from courts, the prison told me that they did not send off my latest mail package earlier in December 2010 to the courts (Court of Criminal Appeal). I wonder if they will start again to play games with me—refuse to acknowledge my mail.

That will cause me some shit and leave me with only one way to answer such shit; at the moment I cannot do much—everyone is on holidays, I expect, but in a week or so, I expect answers and am not concerned at any consequences that what I do, everyone put shit on me anyway so a bit more is not a worry. Especially if one is not eating, nothing really matters then, as what else can anyone do to beat that shit.

And that shit with young Mattie (Bill's nephew or, as the media shitheads love to report it, the relative of Ivan Milat!) has to be a bit of a lesson for young Jess—be very careful of one's mates, as some will sink you as quick as a wink.

So, Al, many thanks again. Stay cool and my regards to all, god bless, best regards and respect, Ivan 31st December 2010.

LETTER NUMBER 63

One Page to Al from Ivan from my Sunless Cement Cave HRMU Goulburn Darkside Goulburn C.C. 24th January 2011

Hello Alistair,

G'day, and it's good to know all is fairly good with you. I am always glad to hear from you, and thank you for the mail of the 12th January, I received on the 20th.

Yes, the media really went to town on the family and me over Bill's nephew (young Matt), and as usual they (media) resort to their usual speculative reporting and that enables them to make up a story. The main liar was that Les Kennedy, a journalist with a Sydney paper. He and another made up that novel (*Sins of the Brothers*) and portrayed it as being a true account. As your mum can tell you, it is absolute rubbish. It's a well-written story—a lot of unbelievable shit in it, but it is incredible as it appears quite true, but it's all made-up lies and of course any facts about the family,

Well they're simply put down, what will back up their allegations – they claim I'm guilty and that book shows it because of their lies, so of course Kennedy is still a reporter, and that shit that went on with the Belanglo-Bill's nephew-relative of mine!

Was an idea to bring attention to his book?

In this sunless cement cave here it is the Dark Age time. They (management) want it to stay like the old times, shut up—obey shit!

Well at my age I simply don't give a shit. At least the cricket doesn't really change.

The situation with me is getting worse; I still dump all my meals and live on a handful of food a day. My condition looks like shit and I feel it but still able to survive on what I do.

The courts (appeal court) did receive my appeal application. I wait their answer-response—it would have pissed them off.

So, Al, many thanks again. You and your family travel life well, my regards to your mum, god bless all. Best regards, respect, Ivan 24th/January/ 2011.

LETTER NUMBER 64

Two Pages to Al from Ivan from my Sunless Cement Cave in

HRMU Darkside Goulburn C.C.

Never part with your inner feelings; some humans will change at times and at your cost-keep on top and absolute control.

Hello Alistair,

G'day, glad to receive your mail of 9th Feb., received on the 14th—thank you very much and may all be fine with you, your family.

I say this as recently one of the main lebs in here arranged with police to reveal a hidden stash of weapons that he had at his home, unbeknown to anyone—well that is how he told the police. Some of his family got busted with drugs and to reduce some of the possibility of prison time for them, he told police for a no-prison time for them he would tell them of his hidden weapons!

The police accepted it! He's doing a minimum of 28 years, so any sentence to run with it is of no consequence; the police apparently go to great lengths to get all weapons off the street and reality make deals to do it. As he used his solicitor to make sure the police honoured it and apparently it was.

So places such as your area hardly got affected by such natural forces, and thankful there are no real problems with most of the people, unlike some of those Islam-Muslim countries. Unreal how they carry on, bomb the shit out of each other, shooting of thousands, and thousands mill about screaming for changes. Crikey in that Egypt,

They had put up with that bloke for thirty years; it was not a case of now all the people all of a sudden decide that he had to go, some clever person led the stupid pricks into mass demonstrations, groups who will eventually take over and no they will run the place to suit themselves. The ordinary citizens think that they did it (yeah, in their dreams!), so as you say here in NSW, we may have corrupt governments but generally one can live okay.

Of course the cost of living is very high, especially some ordinary things like power/water, but one can cope mostly. I was glad when the federal government doled out that extra cash money a while back to a lot of people (pensioners, etc.); things like that help a lot.

Yes, Bill is still a bit upset at young bloke (Mattie). I seen Bill a couple of weeks ago and can see that it is a great concern, and young Matt still not so smart in how he carries on in that juvenile centre. Probably tells too many people how clever he is and of course gets busted for breaking the rules in there. He will learn in time, I hope.

Things are the same with me. I hardly eat at all, but seemly surviving, but not sure how. I look really shitty, no condition and feel absolutely stuffed most of the time.

Most mornings I am quite surprised at passing the night, great difficulty in sleeping but cannot concentrate on lots of ordinary shit. TV difficult to concentrate on and able to spend most of the daytime just sit in one place, in a stupor-daze, no idea of what is going on and don't care, and have no hesitation in handing back my meal for months now. It must be slowly killing me; it certainly feels like it, and no food in cell so I am really stuffed most of the time.

Yes I survive on the shit I do take, but do I look like a refuge from some Nazi concentration camp? The prison management doesn't give a fuck and neither do I as at least I can cope with the place in this state?

My body is fucked but my mind is still stronger than whatever they may level at me.

No idea what the court is doing about my latest Court of Criminal Appeal application.

They received it 7th December 2010, so they have it. I haven't the strength to start up a written correspondence with them as yet—see if I survive this shit, I subject myself to first.

So, Al, many thanks again, and good luck in your matters. My love to your mum and god be with you all. Best regards, 18/Feb./2011.

LETTER NUMBER 65

One Page to Al by Ivan from my Sunless Cement Cave HRMU Darkside Goulburn C.C. 24th March 2011

Hello Alistair,

And glad to hear from you. Your 14th March letter was received the 23rd, thank you very much, and may all be fine with you and your family.

The Warthog, his stories to the police, he has said a lot (I seen the police book full with what that mutt said about me). And can imagine the rubbish he has said about you. Of course he cannot prove or establish any of it, but as you know it draws the attention to you, which probably led to your current difficulties. It's a fact as you get older, time just races away, even in here; I do absolutely nothing—just sit here—yet time just flies away.

In my case it does not matter. I again start my no-eat; I felt a bit crook as I simply leave my meals alone. In my case I really don't care as to the consequences and of course can do more if necessary.

So, Al, do what you can while you can at 52—you have a long while yet. A bit sad about Caroline's mum (Bill's wife). Passed on in her sleep 86/87 years old, though some people go for longer. (Early in February, it occurred.)

I note your comment at a lack of activity; perhaps you may consider golf (good exercise for upper body—swing clubs and it's a challenge), perhaps a local club—you rent the stuff, clubs, etc., to see how it goes! I would rather join a pistol club—at least attend one, show interest. They only go on what you tell them—no police check? Unless you actually buy a gun (that is how it used to do it). So, Al, take your choice.

Perhaps of course you join your old riding buddies, will be better, hopefully that can occur.

I note that there is not much attention to the clubs these days.

Elections on the weekend. Change of government (the name at least).

I doubt if much will change.

So, Al, thanks again, and my best regards to your mum and others. You stay cool, and hopefully young Jess will as well. God bless, best regards with much respect, Ivan. 24/March/2011.

LETTER NUMBER 66

Two Pages to Al (A Rebel) by Ivan from my (Costly-to-Taxpayers) Cement Cave at HRMU Goulburn Darkside 23rd August 2011

G'day Al,

Thank you very much for the letter of 17 August received the 22nd. I am always pleased to hear from you, and hopefully received this mail being in good health and fine spirits (considering the circumstances!).

Oh yes, Al, your comments that you had "forgot how bad prison is, the shock of it," yes, and more in your case as you was unfairly surprised by the actions of the court/Crown in withdrawing your bail and remanding you into custody. Remand centres-prisons are not exactly salubrious accommodations and in most cases get shittier each year.

Well hopefully (perhaps!) I can only remain optimistic at what occurs with you, that no custodial sentence is imposed upon you (so think of a solemn, heartrending plea to the court that society will benefit if you get a non-custodial sentence—good luck!). Though as we know recently, media articles have been regularly hammering the courts for being overly lenient. At least, otherwise a mild sentence, to obtain a soft classification, which enables you to go to a low-security place—a bit more comfortable, I believe.

(I'm still trying to get my documentation back from the appeals court; I put in an appeal last year. They advised me last June that I cannot appeal because I had an appeal heard before—what a load of shit they told me and now refuse to address my letters. I get very shitty at them; I told the attorney general [NSW] grey mutts, MP that unless they return my shit (paperwork, etc.) I will send him parts of my body—this will piss off Woodham, HRMU management. Fuck it, it is all that is left for me now.)

I see in the newspapers plus newsletters that I receive, that mutt "Les Kennedy" a journalist, police reporter died a couple of weeks ago (10 August)—cancer, they say.

Kennedy was a real mutt, the part author of that book *Sins of the Brothers*. (Your mum sent me some pages out of it.) And did the mongrel put shit on the family, and fucken and me lies on every page. And Kennedy really put shit on me over those bones that was discovered in the Belanglo last year; he simply prints up what the police tell/give him.

He was given some attention in his obituary mentions. They made out he was a top reporter, had the pricks like the commissioner saying what a top bloke he was, and will name a police dog after Kennedy ("Les the Mutt"—yes, sounds about right).

188

I had one of his friends/colleagues (Roger Maynard) write to me that Kennedy sent me in his letter what a top bloke he was. Well I replied and Maynard (he put shit on me in his books over the years) will certainly not appreciate my descriptions of Kennedy.

So another mutt gone out of life, but still many more out there.

Well, my friend, I hope your situation improves. Stay well, fit, see if you cannot get any sickness, ills, etc., fixed up whilst you are in their care. God bless you.

And my best regards with much respect, Ivan 23/8/2011.

LETTER NUMBER 67

Two Pages to Al by Ivan from my Sunless Cement Cave

HRMU C.C. Goulburn Darkside.18th April 2012

All those experts on TV/radio say that I am utterly useless then go on to say how utterly useless that the Gillard government is!

Does that mean I am prime minister material? 18 March 2012.

Hello Alistair,

Fifty-three. Al, it is difficult to accept that, a lot of years, I hope that the people that count in your life thought of you.

Thank you very much for the letter received on the 17th, I guess to win the appeal was the best birthday present this year. Ms. Johnson gave it to you. I imagine that you are still over the moon about it, just remember to keep an eye out on your conditions! (If any?)

Oh yes, your mum plus others were concerned at what maybe the alternative was. (It's worthwhile in such situations to spend as much as necessary to achieve a result.)

Bodies in the forest, yes, I am not surprised. Any clever person can put one in there and it's a fact. There is no way, forensic or whatever, can they tell how long a body has been there or its age. I'm talking of when it's a complete skeleton. In my trial I was surprised at the experts—coroners, pathologists said that it is impossible to determine how long a body has been dead, laying there, and then only guess at its age. They can tell if it's a male/female, so someone could dump a body in there and after a while it is extremely unlikely to discover who it is or how long it has been there (no police has ever come in here and asked me any questions about it).

As you are concerned at how things are with your mum, so am I. I have enough aches and pains, wheezer set to make me uncomfortable often, and can imagine the hassles your mum has. This old-age business is really shitty mostly, so do grab everything you can, Al. Keep your health up, and that makes it a bit better. Never give up on training; of course you have to cut it back as you get on, but it still keeps you fit. Keep flexible—stretches are important. Lots of oldies, fifties-plus cannot touch their toes and run out of puff in a couple of minutes. So always spend a bit of time on your training.

I am still awaiting word about my mid-February appeal petition. Of course I have great faith in it, but well aware what I face. No government authority-department will rock the boat and state that something is wrong in how I got convicted.

191

Things are just the usual; they seemly go out of their way to make it difficult, I'm going slowly to pieces.

That's a bit crook, loss of licence for three months; I understand the options with the probationary licence.

Trains and taxis, or get someone else to drive you. I often purchase motorbike magazines each month; there sure is some interesting machinery out there. Hopefully you can cope with that loss of licence okay. Don't take chances on riding or driving.

So, Al, the police I see running around looking for gym person, seems to be lots of shooting going on but really the one folks getting killed is the people that the police shoot. That Norwegian fella who shot down all those folks apparently doesn't like Muslims; he wouldn't be happy in Australia, either.

Anyway, Al, it's your world again. Enjoy it, thanks again for the mail.

My regards to your mum, god blesses you and all.
Regards and respect, Ivan 18th/4/2012.

LETTER NUMBER 68

Two Pages to Al by Ivan from my Airless, Sunless Cement Cave

HRMU C.C. Goulburn Darkside 30th March 2012

Hello Al,

(Watch out for that Warthog prick—he will look at it in a way he can set you up, as he may think that you are vulnerable, on a bond and that shit. Do not give the prick a chance to do that!)

Clive Small, what an arse-hole. I am not surprised that he is out and about, putting shit on me. For months now I've been writing to people about him, his crooked history, especially how he framed me. I am not surprised that if someone did ask him about what I say, so no wonder he gets on shitty programs like *Today* (I never seen that particular program).

And as well I have put in my latest application for a review into my convictions, to the governor of New South Wales. They did receive it, and the chief of staff advised me that they passed it on to the attorney general's office (the enemy!). They will assess it and on their recommendations of my petition, the governor will act on. (Well this is the ninth appeal/review application that I have had determined now. Each time it's the Crown that puts shit on every one of those appeals. So my ninth one may not go any better, either. And that is another reason for Clive Small to put shit on me, go on TV programs to rubbish me. He does not want me to succeed in any application.)

No, Al, I will never give up, say I did it or anything. I certainly do not give a fuck about Carr Services letting me out of HRMU. I do battle to cope with this shitty claustrophobic place, no window. It's like a cement coffin. I suffer badly at times. I think that the walls close in—no air, it's a real shit feeling. No, I will never plead with the pricks. I will send them parts of my hand first. I have been considering this for a while and only need half a reason to show them how I feel with their shithead ideas. There is not much they can do to me anymore, and at my age I don't give a fuck.

I have never read that book *Sins of the Brothers;* your mum and some others have sent me pages out of it. It's a real horror story; those authors "Whittaker & Kennedy" certainly write some shit. Pricks like the Warthog, George, talked to them. There are some horrible things in it. Kennedy, one of the authors, well he carked it, cancer, so that arsehole ended up as worm feed! Someone told me he was related in some way to Clive Small. (Brother-in-law? I'm not sure of it.) Anyway he is gone, but his lies will still be out there.

194

That's is why Small and other pricks put shit on me to cover up things like the DNA evidence, so I battle on. You will never hear or see me putting my hand up to agree to anything.

So, Al, it is your chance again. Remember those pricks (police) will be very spewing at you, so go steady and go fishing, or get your medical issues sorted out.

I am so glad you went okay; prison is full of tragics, as you know, so if you never see it again, that is how it should be.

Young Mattie will get his whack anytime now; he will be eating corn for quite a long time. It would not surprise me if Woodham (prison commissioner) causes him to do his time immediately in here.

Woodham is such an arsehole; he would put his own mother in prison so he could get his name in the media.

Anyway, Al, my friend, good luck to you and your family.

Enjoy yourself (keep young Jess in line, remind him to be a bit clever!).

Say hello to your mum, god bless you, Ivan 30/3/2012.

LETTER NUMBER 69

One Page to Al by Ivan from my Sunless Cement Cave HRM C.C. Goulburn Darkside 8th March 2012

So many experts in the world with all the answers, there is only one way to tell if they are lying—when you see their lips move.

Hello Alistair,

G'day, lots of news how the police are raiding the homes of bikers; the media accompanied some police squads on some raids. I wouldn't think that many people will believe that much good will come from it, a lot of show and not much else. And the police approaching ex-bikies for possible information, you are very aware of that.

The politicians passed laws banning the club colours/jackets, etc., from certain establishments, the city areas; I imagine that it is subject to an appellate court review.

Still no word about my latest appeal application. I suppose I can think of many reasons about the delay, but I had spent a lot of time on how to approach my argument and I went solely on issues of law. In the past all I got was the judges making up excuses/reasons for them to dismiss me, so I tried a different course: use law.

I see that crump had his appeal dismiss by the High Court; he was given life in 1974 or so (him and a bloke called Baker). In those days life only meant 15 to 20 years, but Bob Carr in 2004 passed a new law that effectively said that crump will never get out—die in jail! He's done 38 years now; I'm not the only one with issues (he had legal aid on that High Court appeal).

As I heard it, his argument was that it wasn't fair that Parliament amended the law on pre-90s life sentences— made it appeal to old life sentences before 1990.

The law courts only act on law—if its legal, Parliament makes the law, and apparently that '04 law is watertight.

Yes, it's getting cold. Winter kicks in next month. I can't believe how quick the time goes. I do fuck all in here, just sit about, so keep on your mum to keep rugged up.
The flu or some bad cold will really knock her about.

Thank you for mail, your letter of 29th April received 5th May.
God bless you, give my regards to your mum. Best regards with respect, Ivan 8/3/2012.

Young (Mattie) Bill tells me he gets his sentence very soon now, a week

LETTER NUMBER 70

Two Pages to Al from Ivan from my Sunless Cement Cave

HRM C.C. Goulburn Darkside 23rd May 2012

So many experts are very willing to speak of others, especially if someone pays them to do it.

Hello Alistair,

G'day, I was glad to receive your letter dated 15th May on the 22nd, thank you very much. Its damn cold in here, and it would be the same in any NSW prison; you did well to avoid it. So, Al, enjoy the sunshine with your family; your licence will soon be renewed and until then just enjoy what you have with you now and work on your future plans.

You may have seen that article in the *Sun-Herald* (Sunday 20th May)—the front page and two others inside it. The prison management conspired with an arsehole to set me up. This person Phillip DenMeade portrayed himself as having an interest in injustice and had some experience with court procedures and could access legal material and could assist in my legal battles.

In reality he was just another arsehole; the paper described him as an ex copper (probably left because they were onto him). His shitty story is all in the article; the point is he was not wired up, and so there is no record of what was discussed.

So the arsehole can say anything and because he is alleging shit about me, every other arsehole accepts it as being true. I think the pricks getting a book together!

He actually came in nine times; after the third one I started to make inquiries about him, wrote to people to check upon him.

I kept on about my appeal matters and it never went past that. He wasn't happy and said once that he won't be back. I said I don't care. I never seen the prick for 3 to 4 months, then he came in another three times then that was it.

I never seen him again, and now that story, which is nothing at all, except it shows what absolute arseholes prison management is.

These pricks cannot arrange any project; they lie and conspire with another arsehole to set me up, and they boast of it and have told him that if there is not a change in my circumstances within four weeks. Well then I do what I feel is the only way I know (I hope that I can survive it): I sit in here, mind my own business yet prison management plots with some arsehole to set me up.

Fuck them. I have been looking at a legitimate reason to have a go at prison management, and sure enough their arsehole plan backfires on them so I now work with this.

Mattie, yes, he certainly stuffed his life up before he really lived it. (I note his recent court hearing, where the relatives get their opportunity to whinge and carry on as the jockey for a share of the cash that is given out to relatives by their victims' compensation tribunal.)

And of course the media fit me into the matter—aren't they fucken mutts.

Yes, Al, I am quite aware that no matter what I say about my convictions, they will never give me a chance. That is what they do, not only to me, but many thousands before many others and me that make appeals. If one has no legal representation, he is then rat shit.

I know this, Al, but I still will continue to have a go at them about it.

If I weren't doing this now, I would just chop off a finger. Break my hands, just for something to do. These arseholes do not realise this and think that they are so clever. I don't give a fuck what they think, but they are deliberately setting me up with their dodgy deals, so if they act like an arsehole, so will I.

I wondered why that shitty story on Sunday, it achieved nothing except to show what arseholes prison management can be. I suspect it is connected to my latest appeal application, to demean me with shitty stories in the media then knock back my latest appeal.

Good luck, Al. Give my best regards to your mum. God bless you, Al.

Best regards and respect, Ivan 23/may/2012.

LETTER NUMBER 71

Three Pages to Al from, Ivan not sure how my future will be now very disturbed at how/who decide my fate. All these so-called professional people, sucked in by some rat-bag sex weirdo

1st June 2012

Hello Alistair,

Yes, your letter of 20th May about that ex-policeman and that newspaper story of his visits with me. Hopefully you have received my letter dated 23 May in which I mention a few things about that shithead and that story.

Its seems that in here, the prison management opened up that letter of 23rd May and did not like what I have wrote to you, that I have written to the premier of NSW and also the minister for corrective services and how I will react about that article of 20th May in the *Sunday Herald*.

I hope that they did end up sending that letter to you.

I suppose, Al, that you did see the follow-up strong by that some journalist on the 27th May *Sunday Herald*. It appears that the ex-policeman Phillip Denmeade is a bit of a sex weirdo person, as apparently he (Denmeade) went and seen a close friend of those two missing nurses and extensively questioned this lady about the sex lives of those two nurses.

Even said how during that interview he (Denmeade) went and seen a close friend of those two missing nurses, and extensively questioned this lady about the sex lives of those two nurses.

Even said how during that interview, he (Denmeade) went and had a shower in her home (I guess that he jerked himself off over what that lady told him about the two nurses' sex lives!).

Anyway it seems that this lady seen that 20th May *Sunday Herald* article about how every prick was praising this Denmeade as being such a great bloke and still trying to bring justice, etc. Even correctional services were boasting how fucken clever and wise they were in assisting Denmeade in permitting him to simply walk in here, supposedly the strictest maximum security prison in Australia. This prick Denmeade even brought his mobile phone, still had his wallet, watch and fuck knows what, etc.—no one checked up on him. The pricks fell over to accommodate Denmeade.

The follow-up story on 27th May only draws attention as to how gullible the media was. Originally the pricks had immediately jumped on to print up that Denmeade story, praising him for his unfailing commitment in trying to solve a terrible mystery. And also they praised corrective services for permitting Denmeade to do this, and even some arsehole called Milton, some forensic expert that works with the prison and police?

The police apparently sanctioned this, yet not one of the arseholes from any of the organizations actually thought to check the credibility of this Denmeade.

Corrective services, head office, Woodham and co had arranged it all. Denmeade simply waltzed in and told them that he could "crack" me and would keep corrective services informed as to the progress.

Oh goodness, Al, those same fools who okay'ed it is the ones that decide my fate. How I am confined they have been doing this since my convictions, and what a fuck-up they have permitted to occur.

Services from that moment could only see themselves being on TV. The centre of media attention, be looked at as wise and clever. Really, Al, they are just a bunch of sycophantic pricks thinking that they are so wise and clever.

And the police force, they appeared to cover it up about Denmeade. They should have been aware of what a fucked-up weirdo that Denmeade is, but no, not one word, no comments from them about what a shithead Denmeade is.

The follow-up story on the 27th May does not make me feel any better, as the media still go on about I lived/ worked two kilometres from the hotel where the nurses drank at! And many people will assume that I spoke to that prick Denmeade about the nurses. The story in the paper

204

does not express any concern about me, in how I feel about all this mismanagement.

No prick mentions any concern in how it has affected me.

They think that I am just a piece of dog shit with no feelings, and so they completely ignore me or give me a thought.

Instead, prison management express concern at what I may do in response to all this shit yet at the same time tell me that they cannot do anything at all to assist me. Well what a waste of time it is talking to them over any concerns.

I have written to the premier and also the corrective services minister—at least one of them may respond, and I will carry on from what they say (if they do at all).

The whole business really annoys me, and it's getting worse in here and I don't give stuff really about every/anything. It's so ordinary and a battle to keep sane in it, so I do not give a fuck at what I may do.

That prick Denmeade, what I read of him, he sure has a fixation with sex, talks/inquires of it. *Apparently put the wind up that girlfriend of the two nurses with his weird interview about sex!*

I wouldn't be surprised if he is involved in other weird things; he lives up in Queensland, and that lady went missing and was found dead a week later or so (this about 2 months ago!).

I wouldn't put it past Denmeade not to be involved.

So, Al, thanks again. Hope all is going good as it can be, hope that your days are good; give my regards to your mum.

Yes, it's a mixed-up world even in here as well, Al. Just plan your new life, house, how to have it set up. I don't know if you are planning a new one or buying second-hand, but whatever you have to stay a bit cool. And don't forget to keep control, forgive the ones you really love and the others well!

Stay strong, Al. Regards and respect, Ivan 2nd/June 2012.

LETTER NUMBER 72

Two Pages to Al from Ivan from my Cold Cement Cave

HRM C.C. Goulburn Darkside 24th June 2012

Hello Alistair,

Thank you, Al, your letter of 7th June was received the 20th. I am always glad to hear what you have to say; your mum mentioned that she has spoke to you about how prison management recently told me this. What they said was what I say to you about my concerns in how I am managed. I am basically just shelved in here, given no worthwhile programs, no prospect of moving on to access any program. Prison management don't like me raising it (I thought that they would hold back my mail to you). They did refer to your past association with the bike club. That is an excuse they use to deny you any visits.

Our correspondence does not cause me any issues with management; they are under orders to keep me like they do, and whether we write to each other or not does not change their attitude.

I do appreciate your mail and your reasons for it.

I read of your plans for your new home. The price offered for your present place sounds (to me!) quite a tidy sum, though your new place will take most of the proceeds, of course, and it could be more! To build your own if it can be achieved does allow you to use your own ideas. It can be frustrating, as costs can get out of control.

There is some advantage in doing it yourself, more so if your partner (your girl) is wholly in agreement and encourages you a lot.

Oh yes, doesn't the mutts go on about me; the media feel over themselves to bring me into that young Mattie business.

I seen that bullshit on *60 Minutes* a couple of weeks ago. I imagine the media mutts manufactured their stories, and I do not give a fuck what they say, but prison managements are frightened by the media, so I'm treated like a piece of shit. In turn that leads me into acting one way to show them that I can be an arsehole just like them. Every day I battle with myself not to show them what they are pushing me into; I fear it is a battle that I will lose.

Al, yes, no licence isn't much fun; just relax, let your girl drive you about. You just enjoy the ride and encourage her. Your health and well-being will ensure that you will cope with life in the future quite well.

I in here do not follow that advice. I cannot remember the last time I saw a doctor, and there is no exercise

208

equipment in here. Some people (the Muslims!) run about a bit (between their prayer sessions—they have a lot of chanting times!).

I think that you will see your family grow up as you get older; all you can do is advise them, and hopefully they will listen. (Bill and others had told me about how young Mattie would not listen to them. They tried to pull him up [this was a good twelve months before he got really in that shit]. Hopefully no one else in the family ends up like young Mattie.)

You cope okay, Al, with your setbacks, and do not give up; the cops/prosecutor tried to fuck you over last year but you beat them. (Many people do not fight back in that position.) And you did well and recognise that many people (women!) are going their own way, and now at least you have someone that apparently thinks with you. And may it keep going like that.

So I will do my battles. I haven't heard any more from the governor of NSW, my submissions for an inquiry into my convictions. It's with the attorney general NSW at the moment, so I won't.

Again my thanks to you, Al, my regards to your mum.
God bless you, Al. Regards and respect, Ivan 24th/June/2012.

LETTER NUMBER 73

Three Pages to Al from Ivan out of a Dark Place. A Mind-Altering Place ran by HRM C.C. Darkside Goulburn 8ᵗʰ July 2012

Miscarriage of justice;

Joan of Arc was executed (burnt—BBQ) in 1431 on charges of heresy. She was posthumously cleared in 1456!

Giddy Alistair,

I read your latest letter (3rd July 2012), and, Al, there is no reason for you not to write whatever you may wish to. Carr Services just use your association with a motorcycle club as some reason to write up shit in some dodgy report that really is quite ridiculous in the significance in it, "that somehow you will get other club members to assist me in some dark way." That is what is written down, so Carr Services tells me that they scrutinize our mail very closely. Al, they look at everybody's letters that go in or out the same way; no one gives a fuck about it.

They employ people to do this to keep them in a job or just to feel important. I don't know and don't give a shit. So, Al, it is no concern really, but of course because they think up this shit, it's the reason they use to not allow you to visit me. It's a shit reason, but it is how they act, unfortunately. They are pissed off at what I write how it is.

I am aware of the story of that police person in Bowral police station (who) supposedly shot himself and that things were covered up, because he had given property (leather jacket and gold watch from Germans) and sleeping bags that could be linked to the backpackers to his girlfriend Debbie Francis, who tried to inform the police and they wouldn't listen. There probably is a lot more in it, but I doubt that anything could be found, and it's unlikely that any one will have a conscience about it.

As you may know, Al, that Lindy Chamberlain (now Creighton) recently had the northern territory coroner's court rule that the dingo took her baby—killed it! She compiled a record of all dingo attacks known of, before her case and since then, and showed the dingos are dangerous, attack people. And combine that with her evidence—she said that a dingo took her bub, and there was some evidence of it.

The prosecution at her trial came up with some dodgy DNA shit, but eventually it was declared rubbish. But at her trial it was the main issue, that DNA, and then it could not be proven at the time, so she was convicted.

Later it was proved that the Crown DNA was shit and she got released, so she got all the dingo records of attacks, and the NT coroner now ruled that the dingo did it.

My trial came down to other people were involved with me, the DNA from those bodies belonged to them. The judge told the jury that the DNA evidence only meant that I did not murder Miss. Walters but I could have been engaged in other things because there were another or others involved with me. The judge tells the jury that others

211

were there with me but ruled that the Crown cannot prove it, establish it, and because the Crown cannot do this, it does have to.

At the trial, we argued back and forth about this, as how can the Crown say it and the judge tells the jury that another person or other persons are involved with me when there is no evidence of it. In all my appeals I ask that question to the appellate judges; they say the Crown case was that it did not know if I was alone in company, and they then go on about how good onions identification was and the property that the police found at various places (my place, Mum's place, Richard's, Wal's, etc.).

In every appeal that I made, I refer to the evidence of that trial judge putting in other people being involved with me to explain away the DNA evidence. I still rely on it in my current submissions (15 Feb 2012 for an inquiry into the circumstances of my convictions).

I still await the results from that application; the governor of NSW (her office!) sent it on to the attorney general department for their advice on it. Well it's been a while now (they received it in early March 2012)—I suppose that they may sit on it for a while.

I can only want, but I still do think of how another appeal would be approached. I cannot go pushing the governor of NSW plus her office about the slowness or delay in things; I have to wait on them.

I am quite aware of how the police framed me; there is nothing remarkable in that. Many instances of that is done in different ways—look at how the Crown put extra shit on your matter. It goes on all the time. You fought it and were successful, I to date am not.

Of course I get the added shit of being accused of many other things since my conviction—other disappearances, murders, bodies in the forest, etc. And even tried to connect me to stupid Mattie and his crime. (That I influence the prick! He supposedly idolised me! *60 Minutes* put up that shit.) I cannot do much about moron shithead journalists.

So anyway, Al, I see how you are going, hoping to get away from all the shit and live peacefully somewhere with your love. I am sure that you will both do that, and hopefully then you both can just do your own thing together.

And importantly, do not get too concerned about what you may write; it doesn't affect me. I myself affect them on my own because they're fucking my mind up with their shit.

So thanks again, Al. I appreciate your concern. My regards to your mum and family, and god bless you, Al.

Regards, respect, Ivan 8th/July/2012

LETTER NUMBER 74

One Page to Al from Ivan from my $310,000 a Year HRM C.C. Prison Cell in Goulburn Darkside 12th August 2012

Emotions are not useful in investigations (or decisions. Prejustice the mind into exaggerations, facts, and ignore other facts.

Hello Alistair,

G'day, I refer to your letters of August 4. Yes it is quite a serious matter that you have to consider, it is your future for the rest of your life.

I used to go to her place (after my split up with Karen) every weekend; after some years, Marilyn got pissed off because I always went home on Sunday arvos. I got sick of her arguments and so stopped going there.

Chalynda, my Indian lady, divorced, owned her own place, good job, we got on great.

So, Al, there is a lot of alternatives in lieu of your present situation. I hope that you choose well and I wish you the best.

214

I see today's *Sunday Telegraph* has that mutt Woodham saying his good-byes. What a sorry arsehole he was. I pissed him off in a letter to the premier/attorney general, told them that Woodham was a real fucked-up bloke—this was over the Denmeade business.

Woodham was given the letters to take care (I said a lot in them) of his reply was very short. He was pissed off; near on every time on the news/media he mentions me.

Now he is gone, the government told him to fuck off (he is on the parole board, so he will take bribes to let people out).

I as usual push my case, but the HRM.C.C fucks my mail around, delay it (I sent a package to a Sydney solicitor about my matters); the screws held it back. I can only hope that it eventually got sent. They said that they sent it, but difficult to believe them.

So, Al, again I wish you luck on your thinking about your girl, and thanks for the letter. Give my regards to your mum; god bless you all, Al. My regards/respect, Ivan 12th/August/2012.

Woodham is so smart that he pays near on $310,000 a year to confine me in here and gives me $17.67 a week plus digital TV, etc.

215

LETTER NUMBER 75

One Page for Al by Ivan from my $305,000 a Year Cost to Keep me in my Cave in HRM C.C. 26th August 2012

G'day Alistair,

Thank you for the letter of 20th August, received the 24th so an unopened letter, second one you have received unopened in ten years (perhaps the letter opener/reader has been distracted because he was reading a lovely love note from his boyfriend!)

Thailand—you may visit there soon! For sure it would be different to anything that you know, seen, as Amie (long, lovely girl, dark hair—all of Henry's girls are lovely) says it will open your mind to how hard they do it there. The 21st century is there, big business takes advantage of the cheap labour. If you go, Al, take care—very corrupt police, I believe.

Of course a new commissioner can alter a prison visits policy. Woodham had a ridiculous policy based on his insane mentality; to curry favour with the media, present a tough image, etc., by denying me visits!

I saw on TV some ads about a new program on how life is for me/others in Darkside. Probably have Woodham and other pricks showing how clever they are by saying how hard they make it for me/others in here! That I/we are the worst of the worst (they love saying that!). And plenty of handcuffs, leg iron shots, razor wire galore, the 1000-pound steel doors clunking shut (9 fucken absolute morons are my view of them) on this TV show called *Inside*, shown very soon.

Woodham is pissed off, the government told him to piss off, and he is a fucken tragic.

So hopefully, Al, you, your friend can alter the visit policy, good luck. As usual management here still makes life difficult, fuck me about with my mail, and withhold certain items— very annoying to me.

Police hassle you, seek information. Aren't they first-class heroes? At times their media branch will play up the exploits of a particular police person, but then it falls apart as people realise that the exploits were exaggerated, evidence planted, the accused framed, more people like Ned Kelly than the police person.

God bless you, Al.

Regards and respect, Ivan 26th/ August/ 2012.

LETTER NUMBER 76

Two Pages to Al by Ivan from HRM C.C. Darkside at $305,000 a Year Cost per Prisoners a Year 10th September 2012

My conviction – police prosecution = invention of facts, isolate and invent and implore acceptance of facts. The essential facts are invented; the judge gives judicial approval to make the story complete, so I am framed and this easily convicted. The government keeps me in darkside to show that I must be guilty.

Hello Alistair,

The police tailgate you; they know that the car driver will ordinarily speed up to get away from the situation, then they book you for speeding.

No change in my circumstances. I get the feeling that the prison did not send out my mail to that solicitor. Originally they said it was still in their office, waiting for someone to take it to the post office. Because I kept asking about it, another prick then told me that "it had gone a week before," so I don't know. If he did get it, lot of pages, transcript, sum-up of trial, etc. (450-odd pages), to read. It will only take a few hours; I he detail the issue and pages.

218

I can understand how busy a solicitor in Sydney is (cannot sit around not earning a quid), so I can only wait and see what occurs. I was never counting on him; he turned up on his own and as you can imagine, it's risky business for someone to rock the boat. The government does not risk to re-visit doubtful convictions, especially matters like mine.

As is seen in the rerun of that TV documentary about backpacker murders, my case, it is often rerun on TV, so most people simply accept it.

I have not yet seen any more about this new TV show; they ran some ads over the last few weeks, but really most of (it) would be Woodham's self-promotion shit, and the bits I have seen from the ads is them showing how shitty the prison system is. Who cares, what are they going to see? Some government arsehole saying, "Look how shitty we are making it!"? Who gives a fuck about it? I (am) at the moment barely hanging on in here, to keep on turning up each day.

I told them that I was battling; later at the end of the day, some fat prick came and asked me how I was feeling. Fuck, as if I would reveal anything to him. I do feel I have to tell them with some act how I'm feeling. They have their shitty jobs to do, but it's no good when they call me an arsehole, and make it difficult for me, I really don't give a fuck. I am too old to give a fuck at anything these days, and it's a fine line that I am on in here.

On 14th September, its eleven years in HRM.C.C, and the cunts simply make it harder every day now in here, I have no idea why. I just sit in here 24/7 and rarely talk to them or anyone else, yet I wonder why they act like arseholes and expect me to just accept it.

219

Anyway, Al, it keeps me occupied to think as I do, so I see you and your love is off to Thailand. Hopefully it goes well and you achieve your goals, and this restart in your relationship does really work.

Thanks again, Al. My regards to your mum (I will pen her a letter now).

God bless you, Al. Regards and respect, Ivan 10/Sep/2012.

LETTER NUMBER 77

Two Pages to Al by Ivan from the $305,000 a Year to Tax Payers Cement Cave to Confine me in Darkside HRM C.C. Darkside 28th September 2012

They think that were interested in anal rape/drugs that we're not interested in education, so they mistreat and confine us like beasts in their little cages. They think that harsh shit on us for years and years is the answer, that way when someone is released back into society? Um—that is how they plan it, they say it will work!

Hello Alistair,

I am well aware of how the prison dept. fuck me over; that is how they do things, and in a few days that latest Carr Services bullshit will be on, Woodham and co pissing in each other's pocket, bunging on shit. It will impress a lot of pricks, but in reality we don't give a fuck in here how impressed they are.

Woodham's a tragic, the government pissed him off, sacked the prick. He will always hang around like a bad smell; the media will use him to get him to make comments, but that's what the media does—drag out sorry-arse pricks to talk shit.

I am pissed off at how cunts use me, my name, my convictions, pictures of me. I am one of 9,500 prisoners in NSW, and the arseholes think that I am a piece of shit that they can rubbish me whenever they feel like it, and the cunts fit me up in this airless cement cell and think that I will simply cop it. All I think is to stay in control to keep calm, but it's difficult to do this—my mind is a bit loose.

I do doubt that management sent off my mail to that solicitor; I've sent off another letter asking about it. I'm not so pissed off at him, I realise that no one will put his or her head up for me, but he did see me and offer assistance, so I will battle on.

I see Dave Eastman finally got his inquiry into the circumstances of his conviction granted (Eastman got life in the nineties, allegedly gunned down the assistant federal police commissioner Winchester in Canberra). The informed criminal opinion is that he was framed; Eastman never stopped arguing his case, made many appeals. He was a commonwealth conviction, so on every appeal he was granted legal aid, so naturally he had solicitors and finally they succeed—there will be a judicial inquiry into the conviction, start next year. (Actually Eastman was hated by the screws) prisoners when he was in NSW prisons, they moved him to Canberra a few years ago when they open up a prison there.)

So I still battle on regardless, but well aware that the pricks will hamper me, in here and at the courts. Currently I still await the attorney general NSW to assess my February 15th, 2012 application; they will sit on it, hope that I go away or something. Anyway, Al, I do whatever I think or

222

come to my mind. At least now I hardly give a fuck about what I do or how it may turn out.

So, AL, it's good to hear from you. Your letter of 18 September received the 26th, thank you very much. Go steady and good luck to what you decide on—my regards to all. God bless you, Al.

Regards, respect, 28th /09/2012.

LETTER NUMBER 78

Two Pages to Al by Ivan from my Cement Cage HRM C.C. Goulburn Darkside 3rd October 2012

G'day Alistair,

Thank you very much for contacting that solicitor (Martin Churchill). My main concern was whether the prison (management) had actually sent it; they fuck me about at times on me sending documents out!

Yes, I did send out a substantial quantity of documents (give him the whole story), but I did detail the particular pages that were relevant to the points of my argument.

I am not relying on him. If he assists, that will be great, but I imagine he attends meetings, lunches with others in the legal profession, and he would speak of my points.

I have written to the office of NSW government, inquire about progress of my February 2012 application and they rely on advice from attorney general's solicitor; they have had it since March 12th.

No, Al, I'm set okay for funds, I arranged that years ago. I purchase what I need, no problems (though since Carr Services took over, the buy-up business they stock a shitty range of goodies). I but the papers/magazines, I see that the October issue *Unique Cars* featured a test on the latest 012 ML63 (AMG) Mercedes; they fit dual turbos on the 5.5 V8 bulk HP—looks very similar to yours, still weighs 2-and-a-half tonnes, but real fast.

I had SORC (serious offender review council) see me a week ago—what a bunch of stuffed shits. They look at you but don't really see you; they talk shit, especially as they say they cannot make any real decisions on me. (Commissioner of prisons has the final say on me.) Each time I speak they change the subject (I had last seen them twelve years ago—they recommended that I go into ordinary prison, but then the media started all that shit about super max so they changed their decision). I sent them a six-page letter a few days ago, listed all the shit corrective services put on me. Sorc won't like my letter, but at my age I don't give a shit.

So, Al, thanks for chasing up that solicitor (he can fire up, they tell me, but he does a lot of legal aid work and like most of them won't rock the boat). Whatever—I will keep at it.

Hopefully your mum is improving, get out and enjoy the sunshine. And may you sort out Joe's shop okay. Should be a lot of fun, hopefully.

My regards to all, god bless you. Al, stay cool and wary.

Regards, respect, Ivan 3/10/2012.

225

LETTER NUMBER 79

Two Pages to Al from Ivan in my Cement Cage HRM C.C.

Goulburn Darkside 21st October 2012

My argument to appellate/review courts: if there was no evidence of another/other person/persons being involved in the murders with me, how could the trial judge make findings that there was another/other person/persons involved in the murders with me?

Hello Alistair,

Yes, Al, no one would say you're 53. I look at how you are there and compare it with photographs that I have of you many years ago and no difference. Whatever you're doing, Al, just keep it up; it works.

That TV program *Inside,* what (a load) of shit that was; a few people who write to me thought it was going to be about how it is in HRM.C.C, how I live and shit like that. As you know, Al, anyplace in prison is shit living. There was no way them cunts will show how it really is in here; every prick out there will whinge, say that I/we have too

226

much stuff. (The only thing that is different in how it is for us in HRM is the lies that they put out about us.)

Woodham and that prick Hadley never actually come into where we stay. It was just a shit show; of course then they had that other TV program where George outs shit on me about Shirley, the Warthog as usual being a mutt.

No changes really in my situation, the pricks still holding on to my latest application that I put in on February 2012.

Yes, Al, that solicitor, I wrote to him again, asking him to at least return my stuff that I had sent him in late July, and no reply as yet. So either he is just ignoring me. There is no reason for him to do that, like he was the one that came in here. Offer to assist at least to read whatever I sent him, there was no obligation really but he did offer. I will carry on regardless. His name is Martin Churchill (Churchill lawyers) in Sydney, 0292651710 (mobile 0402568256), I just want my paperwork back!

No calmness with me, I barely cope in here; it's bad enough to cope with the shit that is on TV about me. It will not take much for me to lose a bit more of my mind, mostly no cunt says anything anyway as they know it only causes more shit. Even little things, as you know, Al, here in prison can get out of hand (like I put down some Biros (pens).

On the buy-up, yet for the last three weeks all I get is a note saying out of stock, I raised it with the screws in here, so when last Friday my shit turned up (buy-up—I purchased biscuits, noodles, drink, shampoo, envelopes, shit like that) and again no pens. I get shitty about it, because I don't know if it's the screws here (head office,

227

etc., government) fucking me about, stop me writing to people!

I raved and ranted to the screws that delivered the buy-ups (our buy-ups are about the only thing anyone in here in prison looks forward to! They gave me a couple of Biros. I was going to write to Sydney about it—write it in blood, cut into myself to get some blood. It's shit like that gets out of control.

It's a bit crazy in my thinking.

The Warthog, yes, I can understand how your mum feels about him, like he would sell out Bodge's place if he had half a chance. I do not sit here wondering all the time about the prick. It's only when I see him on TV shows or read of him, your letters of your mum, I'm well aware of what a mutt he is, as you say, Al, he is a dangerous prick in that he will call the cops and say anything.

About that solicitor Martin Churchill, he is supposedly a reasonable, competent person, but gets a lot of legal aid work. I would not be surprised if he was given a message not to look into my matter. (Otherwise they cut back his legal aid funding of cases!)

Anyway, Al, no matter what I battle on, and glad to hear from you about things. I was quite amazed at the Thailand trip—no wonder so many people go there, and it's plain that you are in control and enjoying life as it comes to you. My regards to your mum.

God bless you, Al. Regards and thanks, Ivan 21/10/2012.

LETTER NUMBER 80

One Page to Al by Ivan from HRM C.C. Goulburn Darkside 26th December 2012

I do the best that I could but my best did not match the evilness that the government authorities use against me to deny me justice.

G'day Alistair,

Not much going on in here, X-mas is nothing in prison, just another day. It seems that the government (attorney general) is not going to act on my complaint, that I am a prisoner yet they use me in TV ads on Channel Nine to promote that shitty Woodham TV special *inside*. Even ICAC says nothing can be done, as corrective services had nothing to do with those TV ads—what a load of shit they give me.

Of course the government will protect Woodham even though they sacked the prick, (he was given the commissioner's job by the old labour government, so the new liberal party government wants their own person to run the prisons).

I'm fairly fed up with the shit they put on me and how the attorney general is just another loud-mouth politician, afraid to rock the boat, getting difficult to keep accepting their shit.

When Wal was building his home, he had Lisa lay as many bricks as he did. For sure, Al, for some reason the women (no matter if they are family) will go their own way. My Eagle Vale home I was halves with Shirley in that. She owned the land, I paid for the building of the house. During the trial back in '96 she sold it, got $400,000 from Bill/ Carolyn and gave it to Boe (my solicitor). Shirley brought a property (house!) up in Queensland. I thought she had paid Bill/Carolyn back the $40,000, never did and when she found out she had cancer, she signed the Queensland property over to her daughter (Veronica—and Paul). I got nothing; Bill/Carolyn lost $40,000 (I only found out about the $40,000 a few months ago—Bill told me).

So, Al, stay in control. Really the only woman I recommend as trustworthy is your mum. So thanks again, Al, keep going as you are. Give my regards to your mum. God bless you, Al. Regards and respect, Ivan
26th/December/2012.

LETTER NUMBER 81

Two Pages to Al from Ivan, who was Framed by the Police and now Prosecuted by the Government of HRM C.C. Goulburn Darkside 23rd February 2013

I am asking the new corrective services commissioner to investigate into the 17th of May 1997 Maitland Prison allegations of escape, etc., and why was I put into solitary confinement when no one questioned me. No charges put on me yet, I was effectively tortured by Carr Services. He has not replied to me yet.

Hello Al,

G'day, potential buyers for your home will always plead poor, that they cannot raise your amount but can raise a smaller amount.

Al, I read in one of the weekend papers of people camping out at a housing estate (at Camden area), live in tents, etc.—do this for a week to be first in line to purchase pokey-sized (650m) blocks of land.

ABS repairs on any vehicle is pricey, parts/labour costly. Mercedes are expensive but will last longer than most. Supercharge your Merc. Yes, AMG Mercs very good superchargers, (Mercedes through AMG have supercharged near on every model at various times), reliable and blindly quick.

Your vehicle as it is, is supposedly limited to 250kms per hour but probably go more than 270k+; supercharged ones accelerate a lot quicker these days. It's fairly dicey out on the roads! Al, go to a place where they rent/race go-karts (take your girl, she will love it). Spend half an hour or so zooming around there, do it every now and again, more fun than fanging a 2000+kgs of Merc on a dodgy road.

Dingos on Fraser Island, lots of them and can be real nasty, attack kids, grab any loose food at campsites, that mutt that grabbed Henry's fishing rod, smell the food on the hook! It would have had him crazy; the hook probably will kill him over time, and Fraser Island is the world's biggest heap of sand yet miles of bush scrub on the island.

As you say, Al, a good plan and may occur with you.

Things rather slow, the attorney general doesn't appear willing to reply to my correspondence as to why the delay in assessing my application. I can say it's because they have reasonable doubt about my convictions, about the evidence used against me.

In the past, usually the Crown solicitors quickly reject what I say and dismiss it, the review judge agrees, and that's it. This application requires an answer and perhaps because it involves the office of the governor of New South Wales, then the attorney general may not want lies being said to dismiss my application.

I have written to the office of the governor of NSW, explained my view as to why the attorney general refuses to act; whether that may push them, I don't know.

232

Anyway, Al, thanks again for the mail, glad to know all is fine with you. My best regards to all, your mum. God bless you, Al.

Regards, respect, Ivan 25th/2/2013.

LETTER NUMBER 82

One Page to Al by Ivan, Framed by the Police, a Kangaroo Court Trial, now Persecuted by Government in Darkside HRM C.C. 30th March 2013

Sane/insane: "Standard practice to psychoanalyse subject, assessment based on known history of subject, generally gathered from hearing accounts of others who may appear to be knowledgeable due to some self-perceived association themselves with the subject or and media accounts of alleged crimes supposedly committed, combine that with own perception of guilt, verdict (assessment! Oh completely sane!")

Hello Alistair,

G'day and thank you very much for the letter of 18th March, and may all be still fine with you and loved ones.

That solicitor I gave my brief to (you rang him for me)! He seemly a dud, legal aid (solicitor-barrister) came in to see me, I got them to get the brief from him. The barrister said he would study it and let me know!

That was last X-mas; he is representing that Koori bloke, the one that was on the run hid in the bush for seven

234

years to dodge the police. When the koori was caught they decided that he was a bit crazy, kept him for 12 months in the Long Bay Psyche Unit.

Recently they wheeled him before the court, all agreed he is not crazy, so he pleads guilty to every charge that police put up, two murders, shoot at police, rapes, etc. Fuck, Al, and they reckon he is sane now! So once he gets his whack, a couple of life sentences! I suppose the barrister can get back on to my matter—hopefully.

Hey, Al, I am very aware of how the mutts will never give me a go. This fuckwit attorney general of NSW is as crooked as the rest of them; he is delaying me, my latest appeal submissions are with him. They have had them for twelve months and he is just doing nothing. So I have to try to do other things to annoy the arseholes.

My arguments are fine, but as you say the pricks don't want me to fuck up their shitty system and they pump out bullshit about ordinary things to distract the ordinary public. The media ratbags carry it out for them, and nothing really changes.

So many thanks again, Al, you at least going okay. Enjoy all things and my regards to your mum (I told her to buy a coat or something warm to take the cash out of what I have, I don't need it all, so tell your mum to do that). Good luck and god bless you, Al.

Best regards and respect, Ivan30/March/2013.

LETTER NUMBER 83

Two Pages to Al by Ivan, Framed by the Police, a Kangaroo Court Trial, Persecuted now by Government Departments

"So many experts give so many analysises and opinions as to what is wrong in the country and what should be done, and people think that the cunts are correct. Most people are too afraid to question the idiots because they think that they will look like an idiot."

Hello Alistair,

Those bombs in Boston shut out the news about the mad Korean, yes, for he was promising to launch a lot of missiles against the USA and others and it may have been fairly close to having a shooting war, and who knows what would occur then, biological (germ) missiles or nuclear ones—either way is bad news.

I read of you going through an alleged red light (orange) conversation with the cops, a bit of a shit hassle, lots of cops search for your car! They like that shit, random searches at times by the cops uncover stuff. Of course if you're on their list, then they will always have a look; your car is a magnet to them. (Lots of wise guys use a

Mercedes!) Often when visitors turn up here at Goulburn Prison, as soon as they drive in, the cops/screws car-search the vehicles and walk the sniffer dogs about them and their vehicles, and often one sees the news that many major busts are made on such random searches. The only way to avoid it is to keep to the road rules.

The cops can access information so quickly now; if you're on their shit list, then all they know about you is all the shitty stuff. It makes them look real important if they can show to arsehole politicians and the media that they have massive files on people of interest. No one will correct them if they are (the files) incorrect.

There is no weights or exercise gear in here. I've read about that growth hormone supplements—not available in here, either. So it's good that you have realised what occurs when you get older, one can be real fit at 60 to 70 years old. But you do lose that muscle bulk.

Your vision, dream or whatever, yes, such things often occur, seems so clear and real and card readers (mediums/psychics) seemly can see things. I see what your card reader said about how your dad appears to be there (his spirit) things happened, papers fall off the desk yet no fan or window.

Believe in it, Al. I do, and a lot of others do as well. At times I have people (always women) who are really into the "other side of life." That sheila who gave me the money, she spent years with me in letters telling me of her attempts to contact the dead backpackers, to find out who actually murdered them. In effect she told me in this matter she only had very unclear messages of it and that it meant that their spirits couldn't settle down because they have not received justice yet, that I was not their murderer.

237

It's an interesting subject, Al, and one can get hooked on it, UFOs, outerspace. I brought a big telescope and would spend hours searching the skies and space for something. One day I expect someone will turn up from another galaxy (hopefully it doesn't fly or hover over that mad Korean country—they will sling a few missiles into it).

I am not into all of life's issues, philosophical thinking and thoughts do come into things at times. In here one can ponder about a lot of things but cannot do much, as most decisions are out of control (things that really count I mean).

I tell you I can wonder about the ex-Rebel bloke in here, you know the one. I've never mixed or really spoke with him, just respect him as I do to all, but rarely do I talk with others here. Anyway years ago he was quite wild, always arguing with screws, put shit on them. He with another bloke burnt one of the front day rooms out ($30,000 to repair it). It was all covered up as the other bloke (plus con) wanted to go to court and trial and call all of us as witnesses to speak up about this place, so they dropped all charges on him and the other bloke off to another prison (was doing 35 years—shot dead a copper). Now this ex-Rebel is the spokesperson-delegate for prisoners. Speaks real nice to them and now he is awaiting a transfer out of here, into the main or another prison. His girlfriend/wife (?) still regularly on visits, see them often on visits. He will get moved out, I doubt that they will move me out anytime.

The attorney general pricks are fucking me about a lot, refuse to deal with my application for an inquiry into my convictions. They just keep it, do nothing about it, and I can only wait for them. Vie asked the office of the governor

238

of NSW why the delay, over a year now in their hands. They told me it's up to the attorney general.

It really pisses me off, as they know that they fuck me over by doing nothing. The attorney general is a real mutt; he is very frightened of pricks like Ray Hadley (radio 2 GB) who puts shit on the attorney general if he doesn't tighten up parole laws or don't appeal certain sentences. So I work out my next step. Might have to do something really drastic again to wake the pricks up.

Anyway, Al, thanks again. It's difficult to see how things are going, as one cannot believe anything one hears and sees in the news. Governments lie at the drop of a hat, police still corrupt, judges are simply arsehole psychopaths. The media try to appear significant with their bullshit analyses and opinions on what others are doing.

So hopefully things go well for you, get a satisfactory to you deal on your home and build up your new place.

Al, give my regards to your mum. Best regards, respect, Ivan 20/4/013.

LETTER NUMBER 84

Two Pages to Al by Ivan, Framed by the Police, a Kangaroo Court and now Court Trial, and now Prosecuted by Government because I Pursue Justice 16th May 2013

Prosecution evidence: "Introduced suspicion as if it were evidence, that such evidence was calculated to have a very judicial effect, in that the trial judge regarded it as sworn evidence."

Hello Alistair,

Another day hell...your opening preamble in your recent 10th May letter, I'm not sure if it is in reference to my circumstances in here, or how it is for you and all others out there!

I see politicians everywhere at the moment, on radio, TV, newspapers, budgets and election talks, and the so-called experts with their minute analysis of the pros and cons of it.

I get the newspapers in here and yesterday's (Wednesday's) tele had half of its pages going on about the Gillard/Swan budget. Apparently no one likes it, and apparently Abbott is going to save everyone. As you say, Al, another day in hell...

Thank you for the letter, more information than the newspapers. The current bikies culture as you describe it, no style, no standards, and they run amuck and apparently no real plan or organization with their always being in the news, raids in all states. The governments (states) declared war on them; one can get the impression the major clubs are a much endangered unit.

The police are certainly up themselves seeking information from you as to who they should approach; all government branches lie, the police more than anybody else.

I can see why you wish to sell up and restart your life away from all from all that shit. I cannot see house/land prices getting cheaper, probably the opposite now with the low interest rates, yet despite it all, no sale for you!

Yes, rather weird that couple jumped off that cruise ship. The moment they left that ship they were fish food; I see the news on it, suggest various things, but who knows why.

Young Mattie (Bill's nephew—I'm the "great uncle," as the media calls it!) and he's 43 years whack, he was certainly suckered in by the counsellors at that young offenders centre (Kariong). They told him that he would get 3 to 5, perhaps 7 years or so, and then do it at that place, encourage him to openly speak about it. They record it all, his admissions that the victims deserved to die would have sealed off any short sentence, so bang—B3 years and sent to Lithgow prison.

I believe (Bill tells me) he will appeal seventy as his muttly accomplice is; legal aid is conducting the appeal. I can only wish him luck.

241

It's a fact the police everywhere at least where people are, a major problem is their communication-intelligence system, that enables police to obtain instant information on most people and as time goes on they will intrude more into people's lives, even getting pulled up for a speeding ticket that can lead to all sorts of shit.

At times the training routine gets a bit tedious, cuts into one's time, but it means a quality of life for better than the usual. I imagine there is lots of good stuff (safe!) to improve muscle quality, and it works when combined with the right training exercises. Once you get past sixty, it's basically impossible to improve muscle mass, but one does retain the fitness benefits and then one is miles ahead of most similar aged persons.

My confinement in here, very political, the pricks (politicians) make sure management keep me in here, they are shit scared of media publicity if I moved. Fuckwits like Ray Hadley put the wind up the state government. All it does is depress me. It's pure political shit, management scared of the minister, the prison commissioner is the minister handpicked stooge, and so I get the shit yet can either fix me up (repair me!), but it won't be in here. I can be an arsehole just as they are if necessary—particularly at my age now where not much really matters to me now (nothing in here to matter about) or alternatively they may let me die instead, but I won't know that bit.

Glad to know that Joe is up and about, active in business and life, overcome quite a bit.

So, Al, thanks again. Enjoy what you love and stay cool, my regards to your mum and family. God bless you, Al.

242

Regards and respect, Ivan 16th/May/2013.

LETTER NUMBER 85

Two Pages to Al by Ivan, Framed by the Police, a Kangaroo Court Trial, now Prosecuted by the Government! 23rd June 2013

Hello Alistair,

Thank you very much for the letter of 13th June, received the 21st of June. I see that you have a new estate agent; I hope that he was successful for you (auction held at end of June). Asians in business are openly polite but are the same as anyone in that they want to come out ahead. I can only hope it went your way.

I've heard of that supplement (Ostrion!). It's supposed to support muscle loss as you get older. Perhaps for a short while it's okay, but overall it's better to do the workouts (keeps one's cardiovascular system working—supplements will not). Plenty of people in here exercise, but no equipment, no weight(s), no nothing at all in here.

So it's worth it, Al, to keep at it. I see you have a keen mate to train with; I hope you keep your routine. Lots of shit going on lately, people on parole doing all sorts of shit, rape, murder, etc.!

A while back it was the bikies that was the big threat to public safety; now it's prisoners on parole. The media certainly beats up the stories on it. Nothing will really change over it.

I read what you say and thanks; I am not sure what most people think what my story would be.

I know and it's no different really from what had occurred with you, Al. the prosecution loads you up, adds shit on to your charges, the judge acts on what is there. Your solicitor then was incompetent and you end up with a sentence; Solicitor Leigh Johnson saves the day. You were lucky, Al, and I am glad for you.

My story is no different than yours, Al, and hopefully it will come out. I tell it to a person for a while now, though I fear that he will not believe me. That such things did occur as I have said, I may convince him yet. He does know what to do. I am of course wary of him but not concerned really, as there is so much shit put on me over many years, so now I never give a fuck what goes on!

At the moment the NSW attorney general is fucking me about; it is pushing me beyond my limits, but I got no hope without my documentation, so I will act as I should!

I've never asked before, Al, if you are hooked up to the Net/website with your computer. If so, see if you can access the Court of Criminal Appeal judgement on Gordon Woods (24th February 2012)—only be a few pages. That

245

appeal case is similar to my circumstances except Woods was successful because he had a legal team behind him!

So, Al, thanks again. Keep an eye on your mum, god bless you, Al.

Regards and respect, Ivan 23/6/2013.

LETTER NUMBER 86

Two Pages to Al by Ivan. The Longer I Live, the Longer my Sentence is. 28ᵗʰ August 2013

Whether it's politics or gang shootings or whatever, there is always some big-mouth prick that tells us the whys it has occurred and why the person/persons done it. Were all lucky such people use up our oxygen to tell us what is wrong!

Hello Alistair,

G'day, a recent letter from Bill and Carolyn said that the police went and spoke to young Matt's mum (Deb) at Bargo; they were inquiring into those bones/skeletal remains found in Belanglo forest a few years ago! Supposedly been there ten years or so, so the police ask Deb, "What was Matt like ten years ago?" Deb said he was eight years old then! Stupid cops.

Thank you for the letter of 20th August; yes, some days it is very cold here, but I'm in a building, don't go outside, plus I keep well rugged up.

Perhaps once you move the gang squad will not see you again!

Of course running red lights happens; sometimes it's easier to accelerate (easy for a AMG Merc) but can cause more issues, especially if police see it's a bit of a risk is a crooked cop can easily set you up. Plant stuff!

Your future plans! Stay there for a while then move elsewhere. Well who knows how or what you will like then—at least it's easier to sell on up market home. As people who purchase them can generally raise the funds and want such a place in a particular good area, it's good to keep looking ahead and knowing it will work out okay.

For sure it's difficult to get enthusiastic about fitness and exercise when one feels a bit crook. It's okay to have a break, no good overworking a crook/sore part.

But smoking will drag you back. Yes, it's a relief to have a smoke—good feeling. As you know, Al, they're not conducive to good health; hopefully you can find an alternative. Exercise is one way!

Another gold dredge, may it be worth it, price of gold always keeps up. And I suppose there are certain areas where it can be in creeks-waterways and you would know all that and great that Jess has an interest as well.

And Joe is going good both in health and business, shop busy, lots of Harleys to work on. Glad he's persevered when times were tough, bet he is glad that you there to step in at times, Al.

I see that old USA company name "Indian Motorcycles" is now resurrected and being sold-advertised in Australia, I suppose they were okay in the old days, but now it's just a famous name on a machine, but I see they follow the Harley way, and probably more potential business for Joe.

248

Currently now, it takes a gang shoot up to get the politicians from the front-page news. They do carry on a bit, and I suppose it's fair enough.

People getting killed—what about that bloke, he was shot and survived but seemly just went on doing his own thing and gets whacked for good then! His destiny was sure set! And the cops desperate to arrest someone for the media to see that they are on the job.

I've sent another application to the Supreme Court, ask for an inquiry into my convictions, I spent some time on it but they make up excuses to knock me back on the others so I can hardly expect much, but I refuse to give it up. I'm sure when they do get it (540-odd pages) it will piss them off that I keep at them.

So, Al, as usual you keep me informed on things. Thanks a lot for that, and again good luck with you and your girl, I do hope it ends up good for you no matter how your final decision goes. But stay cool, my regards to your mum and others. God bless you, Al.

Regards, respect, Ivan 28th/August/2013

LETTER NUMBER 87

Two pages to Al by Ivan Framed by the Police, a Kangaroo Court Trial and new Prosecution by the Government. 22nd October 2013

Hello Alistair,

Another sad happening for all of us, Al. Bodge gone. I wish I could have took his place and he continue on in this world; he was the youngest and should have been the one to see us all off. Even in here I will miss his presence, in that knowing he is not there anymore, nothing at the moment, I exist in matter only. The inside spirit has gone from me.

Yes, Al, I gather that all of us are at this time. I suppose the one thing is to accept what we have in life. I talked to Bill on the phone and he told me how it was for Bodge, his condition and what happened.

Thank you for the letter, Al. I guess it will take a while for you to move into your home, establish where all your gear and stuff will go and of course, the ubiquitous shed in the backyard a necessary part of a home. Congratulations in achieving another of your goal in life, a new place, and may the other things follow.

Nine years for an AK-47 and some drugs (your friend's sentence). Unfortunately these days such things will get a big sentence, one only needs a good mouthpiece to plead an excuse for a lower sentence on such occasions.

Bikies, crikey the way the state governments are carrying on about the bikies, it's as if it's a declaration of war. I think some premiers especially that prick in Queensland, he goes on about bikie gangs to get some media attention and he certainly has got some, slap on high sentences if one is a bikie. Build special prisons—no TV, issue pink-coloured clothing, what an absolute moron. The media goes on about bikies as it makes good headlines, but in reality they are doing what they have always done— some get out of control and do idiotic acts. I see this shit on the news, but the media reports a lot of shit stuff just to create some sensationalism. The clever ones will always be around!

My appeal actually today. I received a copy of the DPP/Crown's response to my submissions; they have made up a twelve-page typed submission to argue against my argument (I had put in a ten-page submission). They of course put shit on me, but I can see a sense of desperation in what they say; they actually say that I am saying that the Crown should prove its case and try and jumble up my argument. All my argument (appeal) is "that any evidence put to the jury has to be proven it is a fundamental point in any criminal trial." They keep referring to the Crown case, that the crown Case was "that there was either one person alone or alternatively there was me with another person or others involved in the murders."

251

The crown said that it could not prove one or other that it did not know! My problem was the judge came up with his own ideas and told them to act on those ideas as proof of my guilt! So my argument is, not what the Crown case is or was, or what the judge said, but I argue that fundamental point in a criminal trial is that proof of guilt has to be established if it is put to a jury! As being proof of guilt.

Well it wasn't and so simply saying this is the Crown case and make up a reasonable story and tell the jury to convict on it is not correct law!

This shit sent to me today by the DPP/Crown, cannot. Does not address my argument, it refers to what the judge said in his sentencing comments and what the appeal court has said and what the judges has said in my last five applications to the Supreme Court.

No, Al, my argument/appeal relies on the main point in a trial; the evidence has to be proven. Instead of just saying it.

I suppose seeing how I received this shit today from the Crown/DPP, then the matter must be close to being dealt with.

I'm glad your mum is okay; of course the passing of Dave is a real heartache for her. That is a sorrow by anyone that loses a loved one. I just hope she copes as we have to.

Your health issue, Al, getting a scan, I can understand that process. About two years ago, the prison sent me (heavy escort, chains, etc.) to Goulburn Hospital for a scan on stomach, found nothing, then sent me down to Sydney and put me in one of those round things. It sorta revolves

252

around me, sends laser-micro beams, supposably can detect any anomalies inside one's body. Only took a few minutes for this test, apparently found nothing—no one ever said anything to me.

So yes, Al, it's worth it, those scans. I hope it went well.

I thank you again; enjoy your new home and those you love, my regards to your mum (I have her in my heart as well).

LETTER NUMBER 88

Two Pages to Al from Ivan, Framed by the Police as incompetent Trial Judge and Prosecution by Corrupt Officials Condemn one of my Appeals. 17th November 2013

"The Court of Criminal Appeal made up reasons why Paul Onions must have been mistaken in his evidence that he gave in describing the motor vehicle and on those reasons the appeal court dismissed my appeal and further said the Crown case was strong and Paul Onions' identification evidence against the accused was significant in its detail."

Hello Alistair,

Yes, that's the thing, Al, as your mum said, we will never see Bodge ever again—that is a heartache which will never go away.

I am very aware of what a mongrel the Warthog is, and yes he wouldn't hesitate to put the police onto you, and I guess he feels he has a walk-up start to acquire everything because he had moved in at Bodge's place. I would expect the prick to try to pull some scam to rip everyone off. I can picture him working on how to do it, but unlikely he can. At least once the place is sold off then he will disappear.

No one will see him ever again, yet no one will feel sad at that.

Crikey, it's all I see on the news lately—police busting people. Bikies and those gangs 4 life lebs (they seem rather stupid how they act). I don't take much notice of what I see in the media about the police and what they say. These days it's mainly all news of how clever or how brave they are. But those bikie gun laws seemly very specific to only operate against bikies; they don't need a warrant conducting a search on bikies—that means only one can be searched. I guess that the bikie clubs will change their ways, new ideas and that may be doing the trick.

My appeal application for an inquiry into my convictions. That argument that I rely on is the heart of the criminal trial that more than words have to be the evidence.

I await for the judge's decision; of course I know they pull all stops out. The argument I put was what occur in my trial, the Crown solicitor reply doesn't go near it, they rely on the shitty judgements given by judges from my previous appeal-applications.

I feel that a dismissal of my appeal application will be the result but perhaps that rejection may allow me to go to the High Court again. I cannot go to the High Court of Australia on the basis that my appeal was dismissed (appeal applications are classed as non-judicial hearings, not public, despite a judge sitting on it), but perhaps on a
"Question of law" I may be able to, so I will see.

Perhaps if Leigh Johnson ever wishes to do a book, then I could give her a foundation of a good story. Her name alone would attract many readers' interest, and she is not frightened of the cops.

Anyway, Al, on the house matter, I think that Bill is on top of it. He is aware of what a shithead the Warthog is and will make sure that he does not get one cent more than he is supposed to.

I imagine that it will take some time to fully deal with it, yet the family I hear are already concerned, I hope that all can work this out together.

So thanks again, Al. Your letter of 10th November was received the 16th—you stay cool. My regards to your mum, god bless you, Al.

Rebel-con is out of this place, sent him out to the main place.

Regards, respect, Ivan 17th/11/2013.

LETTER NUMBER 89

Two Pages to Al by Ivan, Framed by the Police, a Kangaroo Court Trial and Official Pricks Persecute me

"Government/ministers, no respect or honour, arseholes ignore it to gain more social status by being bigger arseholes than they normally are."

Hello Alistair,

Your two letters of 27th November received on the 4th December, thank you very much. I see how you are pushing my case to your solicitor friend. I certainly appreciate it, Al, and even if it only gets them thinking of it, that's okay—as most would simply not give it any thought in that they put it in the "too hard basket." They know how the system works, that in any major trial where the evidence is doubtful, but the public interest can make up for the lack of evidence. Sensational news is opiate (drugs) for the masses; the public is steered by the big headlines of shock horror into a group mentality. They fall into despite the evidence is/was equivocal, open textured- ambiguous.

When the media hammer out headlines, it is because the evidence is dodgy to get rid of any uncertainty of guilt, so the media attention gets intense; otherwise their corrupt system couldn't work otherwise.

257

Anyway, we can only see what does occur, Al. At times their corrupt system is overcome, I am certainly trying to bring it undone, and any assistance that may come my way I certainly appreciate it.

A lot more police presence today, I see this on the news. It's either bikie gangs or the lebs that get the headlines, the media pricks rave on about it, the government minister's panic and orders the police to hassle them. So they are out in force, just is clever, Al.

The Warthog, yes, he is a deadly prick, in that he will send the police to hassle anyone and especially on you, as he will refer to your past association with bikies, etc. At least once that house is sold off then he will move on. I cannot see anyone in the family letting him move in.

Some may talk with him, I believe, but I doubt he will find a home with them; even George who is a fucken mutt himself would hardly take him in. I certainly don't take much notice of him; he has said a lot about me, but he cannot support his lies with more lies. It did get him some cash years ago, but now he is one with the problems, and who knows, Al. Sometime soon you can/may get the chance to fuck him about.

At the moment not much happening here with me, the courts! May consider my case soon or be real pricks and just ignore it. Sit on it. Carr Services seemly too frightened to move me on—worry about media going on if I'm moved from here. I will probably have to do some hard action to wake them up.

Hopefully your mum is going okay and all in your family, I thank you again, Al, for your work on my behalf,

258

and May you and your girl be happy and all have a good X-mas (yes, it's all bullshit—but it's in our faces now).

God bless you. Al. Go well and best regards and respect, Ivan 6th December 2013.

LETTER NUMBER 90

One Page to Al by Ivan, Framed by the Police, a corrupt Court System and Officialdom covers it all up

I cannot be concerned at what others may think of me. They do not display brightness and when they see it in others, they get afraid because they fear others may see it!

Hello Alistair,

Yes it's difficult to think about George without boiling over, and I can easily imagine him at Bodge's old place, ratting through everything and not giving a thought of how sad the circumstances were. I am sure it was so heartbreaking for your mum to be cleaning up the mess, and there is George being an arsehole.

So, Al, thanks for the mail and am glad to see all is okay with you. Yes, it did get rather warm here for a week or so and very difficult to cope with it, I hope that your mum was okay during it.

I am not surprised that the Warthog left the place a mess—it's his way. At least now it's all cleared up and hopefully a good sale will soon follow.

A lot of shit on the news about this one punch hit (king hit). And now new rules, laws to be applied. (If you don't use a king hit in here, then the other prick will). Of course it's all media driven, and soon the pricks will be harping on some new shit.

I sent in some more submissions to the courts; it was in reply to the Crown solicitor submissions that they sent in against my application. I have no idea when it will be dealt with. I know that they fuck me around a lot, delays, and go slow, they want me appealing it will fuck up their corrupt system so they make up lies to cover it up.

And on top of their lies, they structure their rules so that no one can appeal to the courts over their lies; it's a shitty corrupt system.

At a first look at their judgements, it does seem very wise and correct. But they rely on the prestige and position that the judge has as having people simply accepting what they say and of course on me, my appeals, they refer to the seriousness of the charges and say how strong the Crown case is, so all I can do is keep up what I do, Al.

The people in charge here make my life difficult and are forcing me to do things that is not good for my health; I probably will lose my control soon enough!

So, Al, you stay cool and enjoy your home. My regards to your mum.

God bless you, Al.

Regards, respect, Ivan26th/January/2014.

261

LETTER NUMBER 91

Two Pages to Al by Ivan, Framed by the Police, a Kangaroo Court and corrupt Judiciary cover it all up

9th March 2014

Hello Al,

Thanks for the letter, Al. I take it that you have received my lengthy nine-pager detailing the two points that enabled the jury to convict me. I could have written more to explain what others may say about my case, but that would have me guessing at what others may say about my case, but that would have me guessing at what they may say.

The media build their stories on bikers, based on what the police tells them; hopefully the courts get to hear both sides. The media bullshit spreads fear, and that is what the government wants.

262

I see a lot of shit about me. Making the TV movie, it's fair enough to have a go at me. I get annoyed when they put shit on the family. I hope they don't accept any shitty allegations about themselves.

Richard! Problems! I have no idea, hope all is fine with him.

I (when I was out) was fit enough, getting old a bit, work never keeping me fit—I operated a machine. I had a set of light bar weights, made it myself—only 75 to 80 lbs.

But it did the job. I used a bull worker for a while, they work, but I overworked it and it fucked up, broke it. So get repairs done if necessary, Al, then get fit and set a limit; it works.

Currently I'm in some shit here, not eating and bloody starving; they deliver my meals, I leave everything on the bench. Every bit what they give me and when they bring the bin around they see me dump everything in it.

What caused this shit was on Friday (7th March) they deliver the buy-ups. I usually order a heaps of munchies, mainly biscuits, noodles, need this shit so I don't get hungry—prison meals not that great. I only eat part of it, so I need the stuff I buy each week, cannot get eggs or flour anymore; they only supply shit, so I get it, spread it around 25 to 30 dollars a week (would spend more but it's mostly rubbish) so they give me my buy-up and there is only 2 to 3 items. Most of it not there. I ask and the guard says it's all they sent (comes from Sydney). I said not right, he goes away to check, comes back with my order sheet, and said he never looked at the other side of it.

(Our buy-up sheet fills in both sides) and wanted me to take what he had—the fucked-up order.) I refused that, and so they walk away and don't give a shit about me. The

263

screw who checks the orders and sends our order to get filled in Sydney, it's his job to do that. He is not doing me any special favour—it's his fucken job to do it.

It's part of the routine of this place. He fucks up then it fucks someone—me—up. He is not a god or a king or something, and I don't give a fuck if he thinks I'm just another shitty prisoner; it doesn't work that way, Al. I do my job in here (sit here, do nothing, no work jobs in here—they want me to do this, I do it, I fuck up and they charge me), yet here is sheer incompetence and nothing said. I cannot see how it was a mistake.

He does thirty of them together. I'm the only one fucked up! And now I fucking up my health up by starving myself, got to go like this till next Friday the 14th—buy-ups again, if mine okay, I eat then.

But, Al, I shouldn't have to do this shit. I starve myself; I know it is causing me damage. I got some health problems already and these pricks cause me to further damage myself. I'm 70 years old this year. I cannot handle the starving myself. I used to but now, and if it goes past Friday I feel I must do more; they don't give a fuck at what shit they cause and I can get that attitude easy enough. I can just as easy rip open my arms or legs and give them some bits of me; it's always on my mind and this shit pushes me into it.

So this is how it is at the moment with me—I hope I survive this bit of shit. Its fucken scary enough in this cement box, then to try to survive in it whilst starving.

I expect some word soon from the courts; it generally takes them around six months to refuse me and it's around that now.

264

I see what you say, Al. Of course it's difficult, they make it like that. I certainly appreciate your thoughts even, and, well, whatever else. My regards to your mum, you take care and good luck with Anna.

God bless you, Al. Respect, regards, Ivan 9/3/2014.

LETTER NUMBER 92

Nine Pages to Al from Ivan, Framed by the Police, a Kangaroo Trial. 2nd February 2014

The appellate/review judiciary cover-up miscarriage. The judiciary are the loudest spruikers to a miscarriage of justice claim; they do not want the inadequacies and incompetence of their judicial system to be exposed.

Hello Alistair,

For many years I have been telling you about my battles with the courts, firstly at my trial, then the Court of Criminal Appeal and High Court of Australia (twice), and then many applications for a review into the circumstances of my convictions (4 dismissed by courts: 2005, 2006, 2008, 2010), plus the two not accepted by the registrars and another one that I withdrew due to no progress on it 2011/2012. As you know I currently have a S78 application filed 2nd September 2013 with the Supreme Court.

The Crown solicitor's office in their reply submissions to my applications exhorts the court to refuse to deal with my application on the basis that many courts in the past have delivered their judgements on the same issue that I raise in my current application.

266

It is not correct, Al. The issue I raise hasn't been dealt by any court in the past; of course the Crown does not wish that what I raise be considered. The issue that I raise is a fundamental point in a criminal trial. That the onus is always on the Crown to establish the evidence that is put to the jury of being proof of guilt.

In my trial, the trial judge ruled that no onus was on the Crown to establish the facts relied on by the Crown case. The Crown case was that "the accused either alone or alternatively with another person or other persons, murdered the seven victims." The trial judge is summing up the Crown case to the jury said the Crown has not attempted to prove or to argue that one person alone has committed the seven murders that has never been the Crown case. The judge goes to say that the Crown case was that there was at least two or more than two persons involved. The judge goes on to say that

It was a joint criminal enterprise, gave a lengthy direction on this, examples of what makes up a joint criminal enterprise, tells the jury that they had to be satisfied that the Crown had established that the accused had participated with another or other persons in each of the murders. (I sit there listening and wondering how he could say that, as there was no evidence giving of accomplice/accomplices, no police evidence, the Crown did not ask anyone in the trial about it.)

The Crown (jury absent) asks the judge to redirect the jury about the joint criminal enterprise case, in that he does not know if there was another or others involved, said he was concerned that the jury had to think that there must be two or three or more involved in the murders. He asked the judge could he tell the jury that or that "the accused committed the seven murders alone."

267

The judge says, "You never attempted to prove the accused was alone." The Crown (Tedeschi sc) says tell them that I either did it alone or with another or other persons in a criminal enterprise.

The judge redirects the jury, says the Crown has made it abundantly clear that he does not know if the accused acted alone or in company, if I mention a joint criminal enterprise, I mean either alone or with another or others. The Crown case is the accused either acted alone or with another person or other persons in each of the seven murders.

The judge put a number of Crown cases to the jury. The Crown primary case is that the one person, either alone or with another or others, was involved in the murder of all seven victims and the accused was that person.

And the Crown's alternative case (if the jury is undecided, alibi, etc.) excludes the possibility that just one person alone committed the seven murders. A small group involved. Two or more than two persons involved. Crown unable to say how many. Or if this group constant, some may have been involved in all the murders or some or one. The accused was involved in all of the murders.

The judge directs the jury that the DNA evidence (11 head hairs) found in the hand of Joanne Walters does not implicate the accused (or any Milt family members) and says: "You may wonder how it means the accused was not involved in the murder of Joanne Walters."

(Quote: *The Sun-Herald*, 14/9/1997)
(Milat referred to the DNA report...this report that tested my blood and my hair against the 11-14 strands of hair found clasped in the English girl's hands...it at the last moment was declared flawed and the hairs and stuff was

268

lost-missing-destroyed, the report was never put to the jury.)

You may think it means only that Joanne Walters was not subdued by the accused but it does not mean that he was not there subduing Caroline Clark or performing some other function in that criminal enterprise. The judge certainly cemented the idea that there definitely was a group—two or more involved and that I was part of that group.

The worst thing in all this was that the jury was not required to consider-deliberate, to be satisfied that the Crown had established that this group existed or that I participated with them. The trial judge used an extraordinary reason to direct the jury that no onus or burden of proof was on the Crown to establish its Crown cases.

The judge says the Crown does not know if I acted alone or in company and was not arguing for one over the other, so the jury does not have to decide if I actually murdered anyone.

Or if I participated with another or others in the murders. The judge decided all this for the jury. We argued against the no onus on the Crown to establish its Crown case on a number of occasions, the following is an example of how it went:

Martin (defence council): "Although saying they did not have to prove one way or the other, the Crown's argument is still it may have been one person alone."

His Honour: "No, the Crown has not sought to prove it one way or the other, it does not have to. It says that it cannot prove one way or the other and it has never argued

269

that it is one way or the other…I have said that to the jury, and there is nothing wrong with that."

Martin: "They do not undertake to prove it one way or the other. But the allegation has been either alone or alternatively in company."

His Honour: "Because they cannot prove it one way or the other."

Martin: "That is so, and they do not undertake to do it."

His Honour: "You have said they had argued it was only one person or it may have been only one person—that is wrong. I do not want repetitious arguments, you did not persuade me last time and you are not going to persuade me now."

The trial judge established the Crown case (his reason as said above) was because the crown was unable to, that the Crown did not know and this did not undertake to establish to prove it.

And at no time did the Crown in its Crown case advance a case that I did the matters alone, or ask questions to the police to suggest that there were another or other persons involved with me in the murders.

The trial judge certainly implicated me in direct involvement in the murders—he spent a considerable time telling the jury about me, and another or others were involved in a criminal enterprise.

And the judge also extensively instructed the jury that to link me to the murders that they were to act on the circumstances relied on by the Crown. To use those items as being links to connect me to the murders. The

270

circumstances were a series of items (evidence) that each could link me to the murders (20-odd items), such as the victims' property found in my place or at other places. The gun parts (bits of a Ruger rifle—was said to be in my ceiling-roof area), it could not be established if it was a murder weapon (2 person/victims shot). The evidence was that the fired empty cartridge cases found near the victims.

There was quite a list of circumstances relied on by the Crown, and it certainly looked impressive and damaging, and difficult to defend against as everything was put on me.

And I was supposed to explain it away in a satisfactory manner, but when I had no idea of it and said that, well the Crown carried said I would have near on tripped over it every time I went into the garage. The judge was very meticulous in his instructions to the jury on this circumstance, instructed them—repeat whole list three times in the course of his sum-up.

I argued this: alone or in company, no onus on the Crown, no evidence produced about it, to the Court of Criminal Appeal, Gleeson. J. Said: "It was never the Crown case that there was only one person involved in eight offences. There was the possibility that some other person or persons in addition to the appellant may have been involved" (CCA judgement 26th February 1998, P37).

I pursued this matter to the High Court, then in some S474/578 applications. My argument was: there is an onus on the Crown to prove the evidence put to the jury. Their argument used to dismiss me was: the Crown case was that I was either alone or with another or others, and the Crown did not know if I was alone or in company.

One judge (McClellan) said it was never the Crown case that another or other persons was involved in the murders with me... (18 July 2008).

271

I eventually got to the High Court with that decision; Haydon and Bell JJ said that no appeal lies from a 578 Crimes (appeal and review) Act 2001 hearing (5356/2009, 30 March 2010).

So I still argue this, my issue different now. I argue that the trial judge directed the jury to act on evidence not established by the Crown. I rely on the principles held as law in Woolmington VDPP (1935) AC462 at 481,482/ the onus is always on the Crown. Cannot be whittled down!

Another issue I have argued often, Al, is another fundamental principle in a criminal trial—that evidence given in the witness box by a witness is the evidence unless other given evidence from the witness box (I am not arguing against the jury's right to reject/ accept evidence given from the witness box contradicts it). The Crown case (Onions' court) was that the vehicle used in the Onions, 25th January 1990, attack was my own vehicle, thus then I must be the driver that picked Onions up. The Crown had two Crown eyewitnesses; both gave their evidence in the trial.

Paul Onions described the vehicle, that there was a spare wheel mounted on to the back of it, confirm it in examination.

Mrs. Joanne Berry said there was a spare wheel mounted on the back of the vehicle, confirm it in cross-examination.

In the defence case in reply, I establish that my vehicle in January 1990 was not fitted with a spare wheel mounting on the back. But I did fit the equipment in late December 1990 (workshop records/the manager workshop testifies to

272

this). The Crown did not dispute the evidence; later the trial closed.

In its closing submissions, the Crown told the jury that Onions/Berry must have been mistaken about seeing the spare wheel; the Crown did not support those assertions with evidence Onions/Berry was not recalled to be asked if they were mistaken about their spare wheel evidence and no rebuttal evidence had been called by the Crown, did not reopen its Crown case.

The trial judge in summing up the Onions count, put a number of possibilities to the jury to act on, possibility one: it was the accused's vehicle, Onions was mistaken about seeing the spare wheel on the back.

At the Court of Criminal Appeal (this matter was an appeal ground), I asked Gleeson CJ, "Was it fair for the trial judge to direct the jury that Onions/Berry were mistaken about seeing the spare wheel on the back when no one had asked them if they were mistaken?"

A lot of discussion occur about this, then Gleeson said: if the police had shown Mr. Onions a photograph of a silver Nissan 4x4 with a spare wheel mounted on the back of it, before they took his statement in 1994 that may have led Mr. Onions into error! (4 Nov. 97) (CA Hearing, page 13, line 17).

The Court of Criminal Appeal judgment delivered 26 February 1998 dismissed all my appeal issues, and with respect to Gleeson CJ, he did exhibit some ingenuity in how he covered up a substantial miscarriage of justice. I give you, Al, a summary of his "thimble and pea" trickery performed.

273

To dismiss the Onions/Berry mistake about their spare wheel evidence appeal ground, Gleeson CJ firstly introduces the background of my whole case, details the matter to reflect the gravity of the offences by the convicted appellant. Very inaccurate and structured so innuendo and unfounded reasoning is put forward as evidence, it is very damning, and softly Gleeson CJ unfolds the fragilities about the Onions/Berry vehicle and said when Onions came to give evidence at the committal in 1994 and the trial in 1996, he gave a description of the vehicle in which he had been given a lift, which contained more detail than the description given to Bowral police in 1990 and which did not match the appellant's vehicle. Mr. Onions said in evidence that the vehicle had a wheel attached vertically at the rear... It was shown that the appellant's vehicle did not have one in January 1990, though one was fitted later.

A similar statement about the vehicle was also made by a rather terrified woman (Mrs. Berry). The jury were entitled to take the view that Onions/Berry were mistaken about seeing the spare wheel. What may have been at work is the well-known displacement effect when photograph's used...

The issue only arose in the defence case; in the Crown case Onions gave a description of the vehicle and referred to the spare wheel. He was shown by the Crown in a leading fashion photographs of a silver Nissan 4x4 with a spare wheel fitted on the back and said the vehicle looked like that. The appellant in its defence case proved his vehicle did not have a spare on the back in January 1990. (See that at page 10/11)

Then Gleeson CJ goes on about Onion's accurate identification evidence details and details the Crown evidence at length.

It's at page 27 before Gleeson CJ returns to the issue of "Onions/Berry vehicle mistaken" and says jury entitled to conclude they mistaken, not difficult to understand how a mistake occurred. Onions first came out with seeing the spare wheel in 1994, not clear what photographs he had been shown before then. It is clear that in 1996 trial the Crown showed Onions a photograph of a Nissan 4x4 fitted with a spare wheel on the back (at page 28).

Then at page 30/31 Gleeson CJ refers to how it all unfolded, said that it was never apparent that there was any issue when Onions gave his evidence that I only raise the fact that my vehicle never had a spare on then. Gleeson says it was reasonable to permit the Crown to argue alternatives, and then goes on to say how strong and accurate Onion's identification evidence of me was.

So Gleeson CJ made up reasons and excuses. Nothing he said was evidence in the trial.

It may seem insignificant, Al, this issue of Onions/Berry being mistaken about seeing the spare wheel mounted on the back. It was the Crown's case that it was my vehicle.

It had two eyewitnesses, Onions stood next to the vehicle, told the Crown it was the first one he had seen. Mrs Berry said she seen the spare wheel on the back quite clearly. The vehicle evidence was not a surprise.

Onions described the spare wheel in his May 1994 police statement; Mrs. Berry said there was a spare wheel in her 1994 police statement. Both described the spare wheel fitment in their 1994 committal hearing evidence. In all the trial evidence given, the only evidence not disputed was the Onions/Berry vehicle evidence.

Gleeson CJ made up reasons and excuses to dismiss oral evidence given from the witness box; he said Onions

275

might have been shown photographs of a Nissan 4x4 fitted with a spare wheel on the back before he made his description of the vehicle.

Well then that leaves it open that the police could have shown Onions all sorts of photos of me! There is no evidence, but it seems to be the basis of Gleeson's CJ reason to say Onions/Berry mistaken about the spare wheel, he lied in how I raised it, the matter to the appeal court.

My argument was it's fair for the judge to direct the jury to say Onions/Berry was mistaken about their vehicle evidence when no one asked them if they were mistaken. Gleeson CJ covered up a miscarriage of justice.

Al, both issues that I pursue go to the heart of fundamentals in a criminal trial, yet the Crown solicitor's office and the judiciary make up the most extraordinary lies to dismiss my applications.

So, Al, this is why I keep at the mongrels, while I live I will do everything to keep it in their faces.

Excuse the writing, Al. I need a typewriter these days. My regards to your mum.
God bless you, Al. Regards, respect, Ivan 2nd/March/2014.

LETTER NUMBER 93

Seven Pages to Al by Ivan, Framed by the Police, a Kangaroo Court Trial, Corrupt Judiciary and Officialdom Persecute me 20th March 2014

Gleeson CJ 26th February 1994 judgement;

Would have thought he was a really clever person in how he presented his lies. He only succeeded because other arseholes cover up his inadequacies by being bigger arseholes than he is.

Hello Alistair,

G'day, I did receive your letters, one dated 6/March and the other 15/March one, your first letter, told me of things and in particular your shoulder operation went okay.

The letter 15/March tells me that you have not received my nine-pager (dated 2nd March). I sorta summarize the two main issues that really had an effect on my trial.

I cannot understand why it failed to get to you, only refer to my court issues, management here address me that it was sent (I note it was a long time in their hands—no idea why, as I have constantly raised these three matters to the Supreme Court, there is no secrets in it).

So, Al, I have in this letter, focus on one issue—witnesses give their evidence in the trial (two Crown witnesses, but in reality it jeopardized the Crown case). So the trial judge told the jury that they were mistaken—never seen what they said they seen.

I quote all the relevant transcript—an accurate account of what occurred in the trial position to fuck me over.

Anyway, Al, I really appreciate your concern and hope that you can follow my line of thought; I wish I had a type/print machine. The following pages are part of my issue.

R V Milat (1996) anatomy of a miscarriage of justice.

Crown prosecutor Mark Tedeschi SC opening address stipulated for the accused to be the offender; the vehicle used in the Paul Onions attack on 25 January 1990 had to belong to the accused, the Crown said two witnesses would describe the vehicle's features, which would establish that the vehicle used on that day, matched exactly the vehicle owned by the accused Ivan Milat.

Mr Paul Onion's courtroom evidence given in chief said;

Crown: Q. What happened then?

Onions: A. He went into the shops himself and I just then walked over to the vehicle and just waited for him to come out.

Crown: Q. Then what happened?

278

Onions: A. I was waiting around the back of the vehicle with my rucksack. I was going to throw it in the back and he said come around the front seat as he opened the passenger door and I waited there.

Mr. Onions described the vehicle's features as having a bull bar, the big tyres, the side steps on the side, its wing mirrors on the doors, the spare wheel on the back.

After Mr. Onions gave his evidence describing the vehicle's features, the Crown prosecutor showed Mr. Onions a photograph of a silver Nissan 4 WD fitted with a vertically mounted spare wheel on the back.

Mr. Onions was asked if the vehicle in the photograph had any features common with the vehicle, which he fled.

After identifying the colour being the same, he said: the bull bar, the big tyres, the side steps on the side, its wing mirrors on the doors, and the spare wheel on to the back of it. (Pages TT19-104 Onions' evidence in chief.)

Mr. Onions was cross-examined in relation to the circumstances of his sighting of the spare wheel on the back and other evidence given in chief.

(Defence council) Martin: Q. Then you have described how you got into the passenger side and the backpack you had was put over onto the back seat?

Onions: A. Yes.

Martin: Q. is there any reason it was not put in the boot?

Onions: A. that's what I couldn't understand. I went around the back and he indicated to come around the front.

279

Martin: Q. I only asked that because you made a particular mention of a wheel on the back of the vehicle?

Onions: A. And yes, that's when I first saw it.

Martin: Q. When you walked around the back of the vehicle you noticed it?

Onions: A. That's when I first noticed it.

Martin: Q. Was that one of the first things you noticed about the vehicle?

Onions: A. Yes, it looked nice and clean.

Martin: Q. You mentioned today bull bars as well as you particularly remember the bull bar as well as the wheel on the back?

Onions: A. Yes, because I never seen one before. (Page T106 Onions xx evidence).
Mrs. Joanne Berry evidence in chief about the vehicle.

Crown: Q. What about the vehicle he (the assailant) ran to—what can you tell me about that?

Mrs Berry: A. It was a four-wheel type vehicle, silver in colour with a red or crimson stripe up the side and had a spare tyre on the back. (Page T180, Berry evidence.)

In cross-examination, Mrs. Berry was asked further questions about the vehicle and spare on the back.

Martin: Q. In relation to the spare wheel, you saw the vehicle had a spare wheel on the back of the vehicle. Is that correct?

280

Mrs Berry: A. Yes.

Martin: Q. Do you recall or not if it had a wheel cover?

Mrs Berry: A. I think it could have, but I can't be 100 percent.

Martin: Q. You can open of your statement again if you wish, but in your statement to police you spoke about a tyre on the back with a black cover. Do you want to just check that, the first photograph?

Mrs Berry: A. Yes.

Martin: Q. Today you sure not so sure about the colour?

Mrs Berry: A. Well...

Martin: Q. I'm not having a go at you, but you are not sure about the colour. Although you do remember the wheel on the back of the vehicle?

Mrs Berry: A. Yes. (Page T 183 Berry xx evidence)

During the Crown case in chief, at the request of the defence, the Crown called a Mr. Badman as a witness. (Mr. Badman had been the proprietor of a business installing rear-mounted spare wheel fixtures; after some initial delay, Mr. Badman's records showed that his workshop installed the rear-mounted spare wheel fixture on December 1990.) The Crown did not dispute Mr Badman's evidence. After the close of the Crown/defence cases, the Crown in the course of his closing address said to the jury: Now, ladies and gentlemen, Mr. Onions says that the car had a spare tyre on the back... Mrs. Berry gave evidence... and she also gave evidence there was a spare tyre on the back.

Crown continued. Both Mr. Onions and Mrs. Berry said this car had a spare tyre on the back—I think one of them gave evidence also about having a cover on the tyre... (Crown's final submissions TT 3178-3182) have been mistakes about seeing the spare wheel mounted on the back of the vehicle. The Crown raised a number of theories as to how Mr. Onions and Mrs. Berry must be mistaken about seeing the spare wheel on the back (TT3182-3184). The Crown did not support his assertions with any evidence. The Crown did not recall Onions/Berry; no evidence was raised to contradict the Onions/Berry vehicle evidence.

The trial judge summed up the Onions court and directed the jury to set on two possibilities. The first possibility Mr. Onion's account was correct about everything to do with the accused's vehicle except his evidence that he saw a spare wheel on the back; he was mistaken about that.

The second possibility: the accused picked Mr. Onions up, but not in his own vehicle. The trial judge rejected all arguments against his possibilities, directions.

The Crown case really depended on Paul Onions's identification evidence (identify me as the one picked him up). The Crown case was that I drove my own vehicle so the Onions/Berry vehicle evidence did not assist the Crown case. Now the trial judges rescue the Crown case with his possibilities, directions.

Court of Criminal Appeal (Gleeson CJ, Meagham JA Newman J)
I asked was it fair for the trial judge to direct the jury that Onions was mistaken about his vehicle evidence when

282

no one asked him if he was mistaken! This appeal ground caused some debate, and then Gleeson CJ took over it.

Gleeson CJ: Can we see that photograph (shown)? If police when they interviewed Mr. Onions in 1994 had shown him the same photograph as the crown prosecutor had showed him at the trial, it may be that they led him into error."

(Crown council) Hosking's SC: "That could well be so, Your Honour."

Gleeson CJ: Because he was shown in a context where it might well have been suggested to him that this was the appellant's vehicle."

Hosking's SC: "I suspect that is so."

Gleeson CJ: "That the vehicle had a rear wheel vertically mounted on the back."

Hosking's SC: Yes, Your Honours appreciate of course that if that happened, police did that completely innocently because they would not have been aware at that time. It was not until 1990, December 1990, that the arrangement with the bracket had been fitted to the vehicle, but what Your Honour said makes sense, it is logical."

(4 November 1997, page 17-court transcript)

Al, that above really surprised me, Gleeson CJ saying the police must have assisted Paul Onions with his recollections of events on 25 Jan 1990. But really I suspect it was a contrived reason agreed on between Gleeson CJ and Hosking SC for the Crown, Gleeson CJ or the Crown did not want me arguing about the evidence given in a trial by witnesses, and then without any evidence to contradict

283

that given evidence the trial judge directs the directs the jury in a direction (of law) that the evidence given by the witness were mistakes on their part.

At that hearing on that day I was alone, represented myself, Gleeson CJ simply ignored me and later on his judgement delivered 26 February 1998 was narrated in a manner to deceive the reader of it—that Onions was mistaken, that either he was misled, possibly by the police in his 1994 interview or at the trial in 1996 by the Crown prosecutor. Gleeson CJ plays the thimble and pea trick on that. He is the illusionist that fools the subject (readers) into selecting what he offers up.

The Court of Criminal Appeal judgement goes into a lengthy preamble into the enormity of the offences; the narrative is powerful and would numb a reader easily into acceptance,

Particularly if one of the family with the case details, and then at page 10, innocently Gleeson CJ tells how Mr. Onions give evidence at the committal in 1994 and then in the trial in 1996 and that evidence contain more detail than he gave to Bowral police in January 1990 about the vehicle that he was given a lift in.

Mr. Onions now saying that he seen a vertically mounted spare wheel on the back of the vehicle and similar evidence was given by the rather terrified women "in whose car Mr. Onions had jumped into on that day (Gleeson CJ calls her "the terrified Woman "it was Mrs Berry) Gleeson CJ goes on to say on pages 10/11 that the jury were entitled to take the view that both Onions/Berry were mistaken about seeing the spare wheel on the back.

Gleeson CJ says what may have occurred is the well-known displacement effect, when photograph identification

284

is used at the trial Mr. Onions gives an ambiguous reference to a spare wheel on the vehicle, and then the Crown shows Mr. Onions a photograph of a silver Nissan 4WD with a vertically mounted spare wheel on the back.

Gleeson CJ then goes on to say how well Mr. Onions described the person who attacked him and for many pages it lists all the Crown's evidence until page 27; again Gleeson CJ goes back to how the jury were entitled to conclude that Onions was mistaken about seeing the spare wheel and goes on again "how such a mistake occurred" (at p. 28) and says:

The first time Mr. Onions came out with the "proposition" about the rear wheel seems to be in 1994, four years after the event. It's not clear what photographs he was shown, but it's clear in the trial the Crown in a leading fashion showed Onions a photograph of a silver Nissan 4 WD with a spare wheel fitted on the back—that he made a mistake does not mean his evidence was unreliable.

Then at page 30/31 Gleeson CJ refer to my appeal ground, though he does alter it considerably (my complaint was the trial judge direct the jury on "mistaken"), so now Gleeson CJ basically repeats what he has been pushing at pages 10/11 then at 27/28 and here now at 30/31.

Then goes on to say how accurate Onions's evidence was in identifying me.

Gleeson CJ and co cover up a miscarriage of justice. I could go on how the police may have done this or that (it would naturally follow if the police assist Onions on one issue then they would have assisted him on other things, especially on the details about me/family. But the question has to be the legality of his reasoning to dismiss my ground of appeal,

285

Gleeson CJ ridiculous reasoning is only his guessing or making up a reason. Unfortunately for me, all my subsequent applications about it,

Gleesons' mates minor and insignificant but it really was a major part of the case.

Hopefully these seven pages get to you. God bless you, Al. Regards, Ivan 20/3/2014.

I don't know if it is my 26/Feb. 1998 Court of Criminal Appeal judgement (54 pages) is on the Supreme Court Web, etc. I know there are other cases on it.

LETTER NUMBER 94

Three Pages to Al from Ivan, Framed by Police, a Kangaroo Court Trial and the Appeal Courts Cover it up 6th April 2014

Bastardry of the judiciary, circumstantial Crown case, story made up.

Police plant evidence to incriminate me, the judge directs the jury to act on the evidence, the police succeed in their frame-up.

Hello Alistair,

And your question to me: how's it going? A good question to me: how's it going? A good question, Al. I think that I am sailing close to the wind! I'm about fucked is how I feel, and my thoughts on things are becoming to feel as if it's a gaol that I have to meet.

I still cannot get over last November when some senior Carr Services people told me that they recommend me to be transferred from here to say to me, but we are a bit concerned about what Ray Hadley or Alan Jones might say about it, so they have to consider that.

Well I don't listen to Hadley or Jones very much. I have heard Hadley being critical about the current Carr Services management and has caused them to reverse decisions, and of course Hadley has a go at me whenever he feels he has to be a bigger arsehole than he is.

But I give a fuck about the shithead; I'm more concerned that he dictates to Carr Services in how I am confined, and I have told, sent him a letter by Carr Services and it puts me in an insidious position as I feel I have to resort to acts that will jeopardize my wellness, because Carr Services is more concerned about shithead Hadley, so I don't give a fuck how it ends up! So, Al, there is how I feel.

Thank you for the letter of 27th March, I wish I could get one of those type/print machines; I struggle these days to write properly.

I see that you got my nine-pager dated 2 march! I thought that they must have held it back, not sent to you. Bill told me this. So I sent another one, seven pages, dated 20th Feb.

The nine-pager as you see is two issues that fucked me in the trial. The seven-pager is a more detailed account of one issue. How it went in their lies. I sent that seven-pager because I thought you never got the nine-pager. I certainly do not wish to glog up your mailbox.

I read what you hear, police tunnel under my home plant bugs! I am pretty sure if they wanted to they would have entered my place and bugged the place. I don't know if they did or not, no mention of it in court. They did bug the phone, got over 42 hours so it was on for a long time. The judge told the Crown to pick out the parts that is important! The Crown said that nothing important was said. The judge said, "Well what are you talking about 42 hours for if there is nothing from it!"

The Ruger bolt and some other parts, receiver, trigger parts! Found in my roof area. I seen the bloke (police ballistic expert) come in the front door, he went straight into the garage via the access door, then came and spoke to me and wanted to know how he could access the roof, get up to the manhole. I noticed he was carrying a plastic bag. Garbage bag like supermarkets give you to put stuff in.

So he goes into the garage and 2 minutes later he is back, waving his plastic bag saying, "I found this in your roof," opens it up. I see these parts, and then he went away.

Later at Campbelltown police station, I say I know nothing of what they are putting on me. They (detectives) said would you give an interview—electronic video recording, I said yes, and they said some parts of the gun were found in my attic. I seen that bloke walk in carrying that white shopping bag and it had something in it, and he goes into the roof, he said, and said he found it; he was up and down in less than two minutes.

The detective in charge then got the shits at my saying this and stopped the tape-recording, end of interview. The pricks wiped the tapes, no audio of what I said about that police carrying that bag into my house.

As you know he then said the parts up in the roof, he made up a complete gun, test-fired it and said the spent cartridge cases matched up to cases found at some murder scenes. But to clinch it, he said he came back to my place 3 days later and then found a fired .22 cal cartridge case on the floor of my spare bedroom, just lying in the middle of

289

the room. The other cops never seen it there, despite they said that they had spent days searching that room.

Of course, the ballistic expert who found the fired case said he examined it, found that it had the same markings as cases found out at some murder scenes, and matched the cases from that gun parts (the Ruger bolt) from my roof. So that is the police story of that Ruger parts.

The judge told the jury that they can act on the Crown case that I owned that Ruger, that it was the murder weapon.

The first thing I made up at prison when I found out that the police tapes were wiped clean was to type up a statement of what I said on that police interview. But the solicitor I had "Boe"—he convinced me not to raise it as he said you cannot prove that you seen that police person carry the bag in and the police get away with it and I just let them get away. I regret that decision.

Yes, that is what is needed, Al—some attention drawn to what police/the courts have done to frame me. Ever since I was arrested and convicted, every arsehole is making up shit about me. It's time the real truth is put out there.

As you see, AL, they keep fucking me over, refuse to act on my appeals, put shit on me because I keep at them. I certainly am fed up with it.

Give your regards to your mum, and hope your bike is going okay with those super bits in it now.

You take care, Al, and tell your mum to keep rugged up; it's getting cold now. God bless you, Al.
Regards and respect, Ivan 6/4/2014.

290

LETTER NUMBER 95

Two Pages to Al by Ivan, Framed by Clive Small, a Kangaroo Court and Corrupt Judiciary cover it all up 29th April 2014

Review Courts Thinking all rely on "self-satisfaction that they are right!" group thinking every court quotes the previous court's reasons as being correct, fall into step on a unity interpretation when the evidence itself was equivocal, open textured, and ambiguous, because originally the appellate court made it up to cover up the miscarriage.

G'day Alistair,

I was just about to start on your letter of 16th April, received the 26th, when some more mail came in, including your letter of 25th April. Today is 29th April, so it certainly got processed fairly quickly, so thank you very much for the letters; I will address them together.

Your first letter, yes, I read your comments about my situation, how I'm continually fighting the courts to get a fair go. Well it will still be continuing—a letter from the Supreme Court came today with your letter. They have again refused my application for a review of convictions, a 14-page judgement and which said that I have been

291

appealing since my convictions and every issue that I have raised has been dealt with so they refuse my application! Very disappointing, of course, but not unexpected. I will still continue this battle.

Yes, I noted your birthday 17th April, 55 years old. Yes it has gone quickly and will keep doing it, so just stay in shape. I read what you say about your shoulder, six weeks and going okay, less pain, but a bit different as noticeable lack of strength in it. I imagine it would be noticeable, Al; your mind will automatically send you signals that it is still tender and cannot handle heavy stress at the moment. I guess you adjust your training to favour your shoulder for a while.

Yes, I see what you say, they put stuff in every room. It may look silly or stupid, but only the poor bloke getting fucked over knows it, and as usual there is no proof.

There was no shit there, Al; they planted it, and I seen it that morning. They did it so well, the gun parts up the ceiling, the copper went straight into the garage but couldn't get up in the manhole. He came out and asked me how one can access the roof. I told him by a ladder, and he goes up and said he lifted up a pink batt and there is a bag (gun parts)—he finds it in less than a minute. Then three days later he comes back and says he found a fired .22 cal cartridge case in the spare room, it matches the cartridge cases found at some murder scenes!

But to really link it to me, they find a Ruger receiver in one of my shoes (the receiver holds the trigger parts—firing bolt, barrel screws into it).

So fuck, Al, there is some parts in the roof, a part in my shoes, the empty fired cartridge in the spare room. And it matches the cases found at murder scenes! Yet no barrel or

292

rifle stock found. Why would I have bits here or there, but it did the job on me?

I'm taking steps letting the public know, some people are on to it for me. Yes they still go on about me. I see that ex-copper Clive Small on TV a few days ago; he's written a book about me and now going on TV to talk about it.

I don't think Boe would admit anything, especially if he is wrong, illegal doings. At the moment, as you say, Al, I have serious shit to talk about. Those 7- and 9-page letters do go on a bit. I will write out exactly what my points are in a couple of weeks, so just hold on because I am writing to legal aid.

(They also today, the 29th, sent me a copy of the Supreme Court judgement; she (the solicitor) said since I raised the issues with her a few years ago, she was following it, told the court to send her the judgement when they did their determination on it.)

As you say, Al, they, the court cannot give me a go now because for over fifteen years I've been raising the same matters and they make up their bullshit excuses to dismiss me; today's judgement is simply a cover-up.

Not much going on in here. Recently they said they are recommending that I be moved on. I wasn't impressed by it all; they told me last November that they recommended I be moved out of here but were concerned what Ray Hadley or Alan Jones may say if I am moved out of here. So I guess they're concerned about pricks like Hadley or Jones was real, as I never went. A little while ago I write to the big bosses, Goulburn head office, if others get moved from here it may cause me some un-wellness. Well then a month later, management here said, "We recommend you to go"! Told me that it's up to Sydney. Well the way I feel certainly don't give a shit about anything and right now even less that I care about everything or anything and this place not conducive to good health, I've been struggling lately, legs, back are fucking up on me a lot lately.

So I just sit here and my mind gets full of shit—none that is good for my health. You are 55 years old and look very early forties. I'm 70 this year, probably look eighty and feel ninety!

Anyway, Al, it was good to hear from you again. You take care and my regards to your mum. God bless you, Al.

Best regards and respect, Ivan 29th/April/2014.